BEFORE HIS
THRONE

DISCOVERING THE
WONDER OF INTIMACY
WITH A HOLY GOD

KATHY HOWARD

Birmingham, Alabama

"While past studies have always had an 'applicational' effect on my life, *Before His Throne* had 'attitudinal' effect. It shifted my relationship with God because I've grown to realize how important it is to my Lord that a respectful fear of God be requisite in my Christian walk."

—*Greg Hilgemeier, church lay leader, businessman*

"*Before His Throne* made a profound difference in the lives of the women in my Bible study class. We realized the importance of understanding the real impact of fearing the Lord as we relied on the truth from Proverbs 9:10: '*The fear of the LORD is the beginning of wisdom, and knowledge of the Holy One is understanding.*'"

—*Sandy Howell, Community Bible Study leader*

"*Before His Throne* brings the Book of Malachi alive! My walk with God was renewed as I was refined and challenged to replace my spiritual nearsightedness with an eternal perspective of whom I am to serve and how I am to live."

—*Peggy Loch, women's ministry director*

"Through this in-depth study of Malachi, I learned that by true heartfelt repentance, I can grow closer to God and hold Him in absolute awe and reverence. This is my heart's desire."

—*Belinda Stocker, Bible study participant, Canada*

"*Before His Throne* has been one of the most challenging and inspiring of all of the studies I have been involved in. I would recommend this study to anyone who desires to know more about the love, kindness, and mercy of God through fearing Him."

—*Linda Dirks, Bible study participant, Canada*

"Shortly after participating in this Bible study, my oldest daughter died suddenly of a brain aneurysm. I strongly believe the study was one of God's ways of preparing me for what lay ahead. Throughout the study, I began to deepen my relationship with God and desire to honor Him in everything I say and do. Although most of us will go through some kind of refining hardships, He is always a just and loving God, in control of everything."

—*Melanie Martin, Bible study participant, Canada*

"*Before His Throne* has shown me a greater reverence for God's holiness and encouraged me to faithfully obey Him and live a life of integrity that pleases the Lord."

—*Lalena Shantz, women's Bible study coordinator*

"Kathy stirs God's Word in the hearts of her audience with passion!"

—*Marsha Harwell, PhD, Certified Family Life Educator*

"*Before His Throne* transformed my heart through God's truth, enabling me to know Him more deeply and to fear Him as Almighty God."

—*Gina Blackaby, wife of Mel Blackaby, author of* Experiencing God Together

New Hope® Publishers
P. O. Box 12065
Birmingham, AL 35202-2065
www.newhopepublishers.com

New Hope Publishers is a division of WMU®.

Library of Congress Cataloging-in-Publication Data
Howard, Kathy, 1964-
   Before his throne : discovering the wonder of intimacy with a Holy God / Kathy Howard.
      p. cm.
   Includes bibliographical references.
   ISBN 978-1-59669-201-5 (sc)
   1. Spirituality. I. Title.
BV4501.3.H69 2008
231.7--dc22
                            2007039873

ISBN-10: 1-59669-334-7
ISBN-13: 978-1-59669-334-0

N124141• 0113 • 750 4

ACKNOWLEDGMENTS

God brought many wonderful people across my path during the writing and testing of this study. He used them to encourage, advise, and offer the right help at the right time.

- **Connie Cavanaugh:** Without this dear friend and mentor, I would never have finished the task.

- **Susan Booth, Gina Blackaby, and Janet and Lee Valentine:** These sweet friends kindly trudged through the first draft, offering comments and suggestions.

- **Kerri Howell:** This wonderful young woman spent many hours using her design and computer talents to make my writings "reader friendly" for the pilot group.

- **Lalena Shantz, Peggy Loch, Marsha Harwell, and Kelly Worman:** Ever supportive and encouraging, my gracious girlfriends at Kingsland Baptist Church helped me organize and conduct the pilot study.

- **Kathy Seidler:** My source for resources, Kathy saved me many hours and headaches!

- **Wayne and our three children (Kelley, Sarah, and Mark):** My family made many adjustments during the course of my writing this study, *almost* without complaint. They believe in the project and in me.

DEDICATION

To my husband, Wayne

Thanks for your faithful support and loving patience.
Thanks also for enduring many late dinners
and my long hours in front of the computer.

TABLE OF CONTENTS

Introduction

O ver almost 20 years as a Bible teacher, students have repeatedly asked me what it means to fear God. They see it in the Scriptures, but rarely receive a satisfactory answer. After the Holy Spirit's urging and much prayer, I began studying to find a biblical answer to that question. *Before His Throne* is the result. I believe that God is calling His church to return to Him in godly fear and that the church is ready to hear. *Before His Throne* is a challenge to Christians to respond properly to our holy God. The objective is to foster godly fear, a spiritual attitude that will draw us deeper into our relationship with God.

The Bible speaks of the fear of God as the correct attitude a person should have. For instance, Psalm 147:11 states, *"The LORD delights in those who fear him."* The opposite is true as well. The Bible depicts the lack of the fear of God as the cause of man's willful disobedience. *"An oracle is within my heart concerning the sinfulness of the wicked; there is no fear of God before his eyes"* (Psalm 36:1).

Although we normally view fear as a negative concept, the Bible, particularly in the wisdom literature, depicts the fear of God as a positive characteristic. In fact, God's Word makes it clear that fear is the proper response to a holy God. But what does this mean? And what does godly fear look like in the life of a believer?

For the next nine weeks, we will explore the Word of God to find His answers to these questions. Our home plate will eventually be Malachi, a book in the Minor Prophets division of the Old Testament. But we will spend the first week and part of the second laying a foundation before we set up camp in Malachi.

I don't want us to be satisfied with mere head knowledge. Each lesson also includes questions for personal reflection that will help us apply what we learn to our individual lives. These questions are marked with a special icon (❧) so you won't miss them.

I am thrilled you have chosen to join me. I pray that God will greatly bless our study of His Word.

GOD DESERVES OUR FEAR

When I was a child, one of my favorite movies was *The Wizard of Oz.* The story follows the journey of four friends—Dorothy, the Tin Man, Scarecrow, and the Cowardly Lion—who are "off to see the Wizard." Trusting reports about the awesome power of the Wizard of Oz, they conquer many obstacles in their determination to see him because they believe he can meet their greatest needs.

When they finally arrive at the Emerald City, they are granted an audience with the Great and Powerful Oz. They prepare to meet him. The Tin Man is buffed and polished. The Scarecrow receives new straw stuffing. The Cowardly Lion's mane gets a permanent wave. Dorothy's locks are washed and coiffed.

Obviously filled with both excitement and some measure of trepidation, they proceed down the long, dark hallway toward the Wizard's inner sanctum. The Wizard of Oz reveals himself to the four as a large, impressive figure accompanied by a booming voice and flames of fire. But the show is only smoke and mirrors.

Marooned by an air balloon gone awry, this average man had been mistaken for a wizard by the good citizens of Oz. The Great and Powerful Oz is actually just an "old Kansas man.... Born and bred in the heart of the Western wilderness." As it turns out, this wizard is not worthy of their careful preparation or fearful respect.

Is there anyone who is worthy of fearful respect? Our holy God is worthy. The Bible says we should respond to the self-existent, all-powerful Creator with an attitude of godly fear. Many Christians don't have the proper fear of God because they don't really know Him. In this week's study, we will explore the biblical truth that we should respond to God with godly fear because of who He is.

DAY 1

Fear of God Portrayed in the Scriptures

My oldest daughter is *coulrophobic*, fearful of clowns. We aren't sure if it developed over time or if there was one pivotal event in her young life that caused it. All we know is that Kelley has an almost comical (pun intended), but very real, fear of clowns. I did some Internet surfing on phobias and found a site on which someone had compiled a list of recognized phobias. Over 500 phobias were indexed alphabetically. I was familiar with a few, like *claustrophobia* (fear of confined spaces) and *arachnophobia* (fear of spiders), but I had never heard of most of them.

As I read through the list, I realized that several members of my family have a phobia. My husband, Wayne, obviously has *chorophobia*, the fear of dancing; he won't go near a dance floor. And I believe that my middle child, Sarah, who is in her late teens, has a weekend case of *clinophobia*, the fear of going to bed.

Some of the phobias listed were extremely unusual. For instance, *pteronophobia* is the fear of being tickled by feathers, *aulophobia* is the fear of flutes, and *metrophobia* is the fear or hatred of poetry. Circumstances must be very unique to instill these kinds of fears.

A few phobias on the list seem like no-brainers. In fact, if you don't have at least a touch of these, something may be wrong. For example, *atomosophobia* is the fear of atomic explosions, *selachophobia* is the fear of sharks, and *toxiphobia* is the fear of poison or of being poisoned. I definitely have all three of these.

By definition, phobias are abnormal fears. Unfortunately, some plague most of us to one degree or another. But the Bible clearly tells us that because God is God, those of us who are His children do not need to worry or be fearful about our life circumstances. Instead, we are to trust them all to Him (Matthew 6:25–34). Read the following passage from Psalms:

> *I sought the* LORD, *and he answered me; he delivered me from all my fears. Those who look to him are radiant; their faces are never covered with shame. This poor man called, and the* LORD *heard him; he saved him out of all his troubles. The angel of the* LORD *encamps around those who fear him, and he delivers them.*

—Psalm 34:4–7

Isn't it ironic that the one fear the Bible consistently encourages us to have is one we sorely lack?

We will begin our study together by establishing through the Scriptures that the fear of God is a positive biblical principle. We will not attempt to nail down a comprehensive definition of this holy fear today. Our goal for week 1 is to see, through the Scriptures, that God does, indeed, want us to fear Him. What this fear looks like is something we will work on together over the next nine weeks.

Table 1 below lists numerous passages on the fear of God. Some discuss the presence of godly fear and some, the absence. In some passages, you will find characteristics of those who fear or don't fear God and, in some, the results of their chosen attitude.

To fill in table 1, read the passages on the left and list in the appropriate column any pertinent information about those who fear or don't fear God. (*Note:* Depending on the translation you are using, you may not see the word *fear* in the passage. The same basic words [although Hebrew for Old Testament and Greek for New Testament passages] are used in the references in table 1, yet they are not always translated into the English as "fear." Sometimes, they appear in English as "reverence," "awe," "honor," "worship," or otherwise; so be on the lookout for such words as well. We will look at the original Hebrew and Greek words later.)

Table 1. Fear of God

Reference	Those who fear God	Those who don't fear God
Psalm 25:12–14	His soul will abide in prosperity / Inherit the land / Well know-His covenants	
Psalm 111:10	A good understanding / Beginning of wisdom	
Proverbs 1:28–31		God will not answer / They wont find God / Eat fruit of their own way / Satiated w/ their own devices
Proverbs 8:13–14	hate evil, Pride, arrogance, perverted mouth	

Table 1 is continued on next page.

Reference	Those who fear God	Those who don't fear God
Proverbs 14:26–27	Strong Confidence Children w/ have refuge Fountain of life	
Romans 3:10–18 (*Fear* is in v. 18)		no understand no seeking, useless no good, deceiving tongue, shed blood.
1 Peter 1:17–19	Redeemed by the Precious, unblemished Spotless blood of Christ	

These passages are only a small sample from among the many references in the Bible about fearing God. We will look at more of them as we progress. But let's make some observations based on what we've seen so far.

Describe the person who fears God.

The person that fears God is wise, confident, redeemed, hates evil, pride, arrogance

Describe the person who does not fear God.

Evil, loves blood shed, seeking their own way deceptive

What conclusions can you draw about fearing God?

To fear God is to be able to know God

God's Word is clear: Godly fear is not merely a *desirable* attribute for a Christian, but the only *correct* response to the one true God. Throughout this study, we will see how this statement is based on the Word of God. We will also discuss the meaning of godly fear, explore scriptural descriptions, and consider the original Hebrew and Greek words.

🐚 **As a close to today's lesson, write a prayer asking God to teach you what it means to fear Him.**

DAY 2

Deserving of Fear Because He Is Holy

God's unique, divine nature can be summed up with the word *holy.* R. C. Sproul, author of *The Holiness of God,* puts it this way: "[W]hen the word *holy* is applied to God, it does not signify one single attribute. On the contrary, God is called holy in a general sense. The word is used as a synonym for his deity. That is, the word *holy* calls attention to all that God is."[1]

Today we are going to visit the foot of Mount Sinai (also known as Mount Horeb) where God established His covenant with the newly formed nation of Israel. The purpose for this journey is to know God more by getting a glimpse of His holiness.

In preparation for our journey, read the passages in table 2. As you read, take note of the table headings and record what you find.

Table 2. Preparation for experiencing God's holiness

SCRIPTURE	INSTRUCTIONS & PREPARATIONS	EVIDENCE OF GOD'S PRESENCE	THE PEOPLE'S RESPONSE
Exodus 19:10–25	1 Cleanse body 2. cleanse clothes 3. Abstain from Sex	Will appear on Mt Sinai God answered	
Deuteronomy 4:9–14	Keep your Soul diligent	The voice of The Lord to moses.	
Hebrews 12:18–21			

Read the following story, which is my personal depiction of some of the events described in Exodus 19 and associated Scriptures. As you read, imagine you are one of the Israelites.

Strap on your sandals and load your donkey. It's time to go. Remember, you left Egypt two months ago. God delivered you and all your people from the hand of Pharaoh. God parted the sea, and you crossed over on dry ground. And now, 150 miles further on, you stand on the desert of Sinai, a long plain about two miles long and a half mile wide. A mountain range rings one end of the plain, but one peak is more prominent than the rest. It rises straight up, standing like a sentinel against the backdrop of the sky. Here, in the shadow of Mount Sinai, you set up camp.

Almost immediately, Moses climbs the mountain to hear from God and quickly returns with instructions. You must prepare for a visit from Yahweh. He is coming to the mountain! You have two days to purify yourself. While you busy yourself bathing and washing your clothes, some of the leaders are carrying out God's safety instructions. They are setting up barricades around the base of the mountain and tying up any loose livestock. Wandering onto the mountain, even accidentally, is a death sentence. The anticipation and the anxiety build as those two days creep along.

Finally dawn breaks on the third day. You rush out of your tent at the long, loud blast from the ram's horn. It sounds as if it is right in the tent with you. The weather is certainly different from yesterday's. The early morning light seems brighter than noon as almost continuous lightning strikes illuminate the pale sky. And the thunder! It's so loud and persistent that you can't even shout a greeting to your neighbor. But the instructions were made clear yesterday; you know what to do.

Making your way to the edge of camp where all the people are gathering, you notice this huge crowd is silent. Moses turns everyone's attention to the mountain.

As you watch, a dense cloud descends and envelops the peak. Moses leads the crowd forward to the very foot of the mountain, but no farther. Shoulder to shoulder with fellow Israelites, you look up. It's as if the entire mountain is on fire. Smoke billows upward, almost blocking the sun. Darkness now dominates the plain. From the midst of the smoke, flames shoot to the sky. You are transfixed. You cannot take your eyes off the mountain. Your feet begin to feel a mild vibration. It quickly intensifies. The ground shakes so violently that you drop to your knees because you cannot stand. Everyone around you also drops to the ground, and you realize that it is not merely the movement of the earth that has put you there.

Above the thunder, you hear the blast of the horn grow louder as it announces Yahweh. He speaks, and the sound is like the thunder, but different, and you realize you are hearing the very voice of God. Yahweh's voice is both awesome and terrible. He calls to Moses, and amidst these terrifying events, Moses somehow manages to climb up into the smoke to meet with God.

Contemplate for a moment the otherness of God. He is like no other. Did our journey give you a sense of the holiness of God? In Malachi 3:6, God says, *"I am the LORD, and I do not change"* (NLT). The God who met with Moses on Mount Sinai to establish the Old Covenant is also the God of the New Covenant. His holiness is as intact today as it was then.

> **Read Deuteronomy 5:22–29. Compare this passage with Deuteronomy 4:9–10. According to these passages, what was God's purpose in exposing the people to His awesome holiness?**
> (***Note:*** The Hebrew word for "fear" is found in Deuteronomy 5:29 and 4:10. Tomorrow we will look at the original language.) \\\

❧ What personal application can you make here?

Don't miss this vital point: God wanted the people to fear Him. In fact, the proper human response to a holy God is fear! *"The LORD Almighty is the one you are to regard as holy, he is the one you are to fear, he is the one you are to dread"* (Isaiah 8:13). The reason we should fear Him is because He is holy. *"Who will not fear you, O Lord, and bring glory to your name? For you alone are holy. All nations will come and worship before you, for your righteous acts have been revealed"* (Revelation 15:4). In *The Knowledge of the Holy*, A.W. Tozer describes the result of man's encounter with the holiness of God as "an acute feeling of personal insufficiency in the presence of God the Almighty."[2] When we experience God's holiness, we better understand who He is, and we, therefore, better understand who we are. What a humbling experience.

When God descended on Mount Sinai to give the Law to Moses, the people, for their own protection, were not allowed to touch or even approach the mountain. The Lord said to Moses, *"Go back down and warn the people not to cross the boundaries. They must not come up here to see the Lord, for those who do will die"* (Exodus 19:21 NLT). At first glance, this picture of an unapproachable God seems to be in conflict with the God of grace in the New Testament. But just like the Israelites had Moses to intercede on their behalf, we too have an intercessor with God.

Read Hebrews 10:19–22. Describe the great privilege we have as Christians.

Confidence to enter the Holy Place

What makes this great privilege possible?

The blood of Christ

🕊 **As we end today's lesson, reflect on this sacred privilege. Spend time in prayer thanking God for your Intercessor.**

Day 3

Fear Defined

To help us define what it means to fear God, let's look at the original Hebrew word for "fear," *yare'*. This word is used in both Deuteronomy 4:10 and 5:29, as discussed during the day 2 study this week. See language notes[3] on the far right for a definition of *yare'*. The root of this word and its various forms appear over 300 times in the Old Testament. Its object is God in almost 80 percent of the occurrences,[4] according to *New International Dictionary of Old Testament Theology and Exegesis*. Depending on your Bible translation, the word *yare'* may appear in English as "fear," "awe," or "revere." For example, in the New International Version, *yare'* is translated as "revere" in Deuteronomy 4:10 but as "fear" in Deuteronomy 6:2.

Read the following words in a dictionary, and record their meanings as they apply to our proper response to God.
• **Afraid**

- **Awe**
- **Fear**
- **Honor**
- **Respect**
- **Reverence**

Vine's Complete Expository Dictionary of Old and New Testament Words by W. E. Vine and others elaborates on the meaning of *yare'*: "Used of a person in an exalted position, [*yare'*] connotes 'standing in awe.' This is not simple fear, but reverence, whereby an individual recognizes the power and position of the individual revered and renders him proper respect."[5]

Consider what *God* expects when He says He wants us to fear, honor, respect, revere, and be in awe of Him. Our human ideal probably falls quite short.

I don't know how many times I have told my son, Mark, to clean his room. After a while, I would go to check out the job. (I know you are way ahead of me.) Mark's standard of clean is not quite the same as mine. Invariably I would find clothes or candy wrappers on the floor, the desk stacked with papers, and a walk-in closet you couldn't walk in. When questioned, he would say, "It looks clean to me."

Over time, we developed a new dialogue concerning room cleaning that goes something like this:

ME: Mark, go clean your room.

MARK: My clean or your clean?

ME: My clean. Do you really have to ask?

Unfortunately, even though he now knows what my clean is, when he does the job, it is still usually *his* clean.

The same is true with fearing God. We say, "Oh yes, that means we are to revere, respect, and be in awe of God." But whose standards for these attitudes are we using?

The Bible often equates the fear of God with living rightly and obediently before Him. The two Deuteronomy passages discussed on day

> **Language Notes[3]**
>
> **Deuteronomy 4:10; 5:29; 6:2**
>
> English: **fear/awe/revere**
> Hebrew: *yare'* (verb)
> Pronunciation: yaw-ray'
> Definition:
> - to fear, be afraid
> - to stand in awe of, be awed
> - to fear, reverence, honor, respect
>
> (**Note:** When a Hebrew or Greek word has multiple layers and nuances of meaning, it doesn't necessarily mean all things at all times. Rely on context to determine the precise meaning in any given passage.)

2 of this week's study (4:9–14; 5:22–29) are examples. As you read through passages in the Bible about fearing God, it becomes clear that proper fear of Him and proper living before Him are almost synonymous. Additionally, the Bible portrays the fear of God as the motivation needed to produce right living. The Hebrew midwives in the first chapter of Exodus serve as an excellent example.

> **Read Exodus 1:15–17. *Yare'*, our Hebrew word for "fear," is found in verse 17. How did the midwives respond to Pharaoh's order and why?**

Let's consider their actions. Pharaoh was extremely powerful. He had the authority and the means to make their lives unbearable or to order their deaths. Yet their fear of God moved them to obey God instead of Pharaoh.

> **Now read Exodus 1:20–21. *Yare'* is found also in verse 21. What was the result of the midwives' fearful obedience to God?**

> **Based on what we've seen today, put into your own words what it means to fear God.**

A true fear of God is not a given in our lives. The choice is ours. Proverbs 1:29 states, *"For they hated knowledge and chose not to fear the LORD"* (NLT). To have the appropriate fear of God, we must first choose to fear Him.

Next, we must allow the fear of God to become a pervasive attitude that plays itself out in our thoughts, words, and behavior. We can say that we fear God, but such statements are only words if our lives do not reflect a yielded obedience to Him. A proper attitude toward God will be evident in the way we live.

> **As we close this lesson, consider your life. What kind of heart attitude toward God does your lifestyle reveal? Do you live in consistent obedience to God, or are you more often obedient to your own desires?**

🕊 Pray now, asking God to reveal your heart attitude, and record any insights He gives you.

DAY 4

God's Holy Nature

How would you describe yourself—not your physical appearance, but who you are and how you relate to others? Give it a try!

🕊 In 20 words or less, write a brief description of yourself.

Now look back and count the adjectives. Did you use words like *friendly* or *shy, funny* or *serious, organized* or *scatterbrained*? You probably used some positive descriptive words and some negative. We use these kinds of adjectives to describe ourselves or other people because they are concepts we understand. Therefore when we attempt to know and understand God, we resort to the same means. We use human language to describe a God who is really indescribable. So no matter how good a job we do in describing God, our efforts will always fall short. We must not let that keep us from trying, but we do need to remember the limitations of our words.

In day 2 of this week, we saw that the word *holy* can be used as a synonym for God's deity. The Bible uses this general term to describe the nature of God, to define who He is. From beginning to end, the Bible repeatedly describes God as holy. One of the best-known passages describing God as holy is from Isaiah: *"And they were calling to one another: 'Holy, holy, holy is the* LORD *Almighty; the whole earth is full of his glory'"* (Isaiah 6:3). The seraphim repeated the word *holy* three times. This repetition emphasizes the absolute truth and the magnitude of the holiness of God.

Holy is translated from the Hebrew adjective *qadosh* [pronounced *kaw-doshe'*]. The *Theological Wordbook of the Old Testament* refers to the holiness of God as "totally good and entirely without evil." Further, that book states, "By definition, holiness is separate from all that is sinful and profane." And because God is holy, He is "above the weaknesses and imperfections of mortals."[6] The holiness of God is the essence of His being. Because He is holy (above weaknesses and imperfections), when He reveals Himself to us in word or deed, He does so within the context of His perfect holiness.

In our humanness, we use adjectives and attributes to describe His holy nature. A.W. Tozer describes God's divine unified nature in his book *The Knowledge of the Holy:*

> The harmony of His being is the result not of a perfect balance of parts but of the absence of parts. Between His attributes no contradiction can exist. He need not suspend one to exercise another, for in Him all His attributes are one. All of God does all that God does; He does not divide Himself to perform a work, but works in the total unity of His being.[7]
>
> —A.W. Tozer, *The Knowledge of the Holy*

God is holy; therefore God is good. God is holy; therefore God is trustworthy. God is holy; therefore God is just, merciful, and faithful.

Although God is one holy nature and always operates in unity with His holy nature, we humans still need to describe God by using attributes to understand Him better. Rather than jump around to numerous Scripture passages that mention one or two of God's attributes, we will read one longer passage. Isaiah 40, though not exhaustive, gives us a lot of information about the character of God.

Read all of Isaiah 40 (from the New International Version, if available). As you read, write down any descriptive words, phrases, or actions that speak to the nature and character of God.

Now using what you discovered from Isaiah 40, write a character sketch of God's holy nature.

Read Jeremiah 5:20–25. (Verses 22 and 24 contain the word *yare'*.) Compare your findings in this passage with what you found in Isaiah 40. What similarities do you see?

What does the Jeremiah passage state to be the proper response to who God is?

🕊 **What should your response be when you consider the nature of God?**

Day 5

God Alone

I am nearsighted. I've been wearing glasses or contacts for the last three decades. My eyesight is so bad that I can't find my glasses without my glasses. Before I got my first pair of glasses, I would have agreed that trees have leaves, but I did not understand what that meant or really looked like until I looked with adjusted vision at a tree. My glasses presented a whole new world.

Unfortunately, my physical sight is not my only type of "sight" that needs adjustment. I have been guilty—as I'm sure most Christians have been at one time or another—of spiritual nearsightedness. My own little world is in pretty clear focus, but anything and anyone outside its borders are hazy.

Although we may not readily admit it, we operate under the mistaken attitude that God is merely in and about *our* world, *our* lives, and *our* plans. Many of us, although Christians, have crafted a picture of God based merely on our limited worldview. As we often say, we have put God in a box. But when we move our focus from ourselves to God the Creator, a paradigm shift occurs.

God used a missions trip to Africa to begin to adjust my spiritual sight. Even before going, I would readily have agreed that my God is also the God of Africa and Asia and every other part of the world. Yet when I actually spent time in Africa, I realized I had been limiting God.

He is not merely God of the Christians in the United States. He is also the God of Maputo, Mozambique. In that place, the ongoing discussion of whether hymns or praise choruses are better for worship is irrelevant. In Maputo, God is glorified when Mozambicans dance in worship and lift their voices to Him in African rhythms. Our God is the One who puts the songs, though varied in style, in the hearts of His people.

Throughout history, God has made plain to man what may be known about Him. Humans have believed instinctively there is a God. Even isolated cultures worship some form of divine being or beings.

Read Romans 1:18–25. Explain in your own words why godless people are without excuse.

What practice do people automatically adopt when they reject the truth concerning the one, true God?

Do you think idolatry is a prominent problem where you live today? Why or why not?

Recognizing and worshipping anything as "god" other than the one, true God is idolatry. I have often heard this applied to anything we put first in our lives, anything we put ahead of God: for example, our job or even our family. But let me propose that worshipping God as *less than He is* could become a form of idolatry. If our view of God causes us to see Him with limits—limited power, boundaries for His sovereignty—then haven't we *"exchanged the glory of the immortal God for images made to look like mortal man"* (Romans 1:23)? Paul confronted this very thing in Athens. The city was full of idols. The Athenians were very religious but did not know the only God who is God.

Read Acts 17:24–28. Describe *"the God"* whom Paul introduced to the people of Athens.

Does this describe your God, or have you, due to spiritual nearsightedness, made God out to be less than He is?

God is active in every corner of the globe, working through all people and all cultures to bring about His eternal purposes. I am guilty of seeing God as smaller than He is. When we have a limited view of God, we do not realize His power and greatness. We fail to see His overwhelming divine qualities that, when seen, even with our limited human understanding, should lay us out prostrate on the floor. A better understanding of God's character will most certainly produce fear in any human being.

Read Psalm 33. Verse 1 declares, *"It is fitting for the upright to praise him."* **As you read through this psalm, record the reasons we should praise God.** (***Note:*** The Hebrew verb *yare'* [fear, awe, revere] is used in verses 8 and 18. See language notes for week 1, day 3.)

According to this psalm, why should we fear God?

What is the result of fearing God?

🕊 **In closing, ask God to reveal to you the ways your view of Him is limited. Record here whatever He tells you. Then ask Him to give you a truer understanding of Himself.**

WEEK 2

GOD DECLARES HIS LOVE

God's very first message to Israel in the Book of Malachi is a declaration of love (Malachi 1:1–2). Love is the perfect place to begin a study about fearing God because love and fear go hand in hand. Psalm 103:11 declares, *"For as high as the heavens are above the earth, so great is his love for those who fear him."*

The Old Testament repeatedly describes God's love for Israel as *"un- failing"* and *"eternal"* (as in Exodus 15:13 and 1 Kings 10:9, respectively). God's covenant with Israel is even referred to several times as His *"covenant of love"* (for example, Deuteronomy 7:9). God showed His love for Israel by choosing that nation as His special possession among all the nations of the world. Even though Israel broke covenant with God over and over again, God never withheld His love. Even through judgment, God acted in love. He could do nothing less, because love is a facet of His perfect divine nature (1 John 4:8).

DAY 1

God's Love Revealed in History

We are going to begin this week with a brief history review. I know what many of you are thinking: "Boring! I'll skip the lecture." But let me encourage you to dig in with me. Understanding the context in which any Bible book or passage is written is vital to understanding what God wants to teach us through it. Today's lesson will set the stage for Malachi.

After God established Israel in the Promised Land, His chosen nation repeatedly went through cycles of sin and repentance; the sin brought God's judgment and the repentance brought restoration. Through it all, God continually and faithfully called His people to a closer love relationship with Him through His messengers, the prophets. We are going to travel quickly through this segment of Israel's history, stopping briefly at important landmarks.

Historical Marker 1: 930 B.C.

When David died, his son Solomon became king. Unfortunately, Solomon did not keep an undivided heart for God like his father had had before him. Solomon, influenced by his many foreign wives, slipped into blatant idolatry. For David's sake, God allowed Solomon to continue to rule over the united Israel. However, Solomon's son experienced the consequences of his father's sin when God removed a large portion of the kingdom from his rule (1 Kings 11:1–13).

Therefore, after the death of King Solomon, the nation of Israel was divided. The two southern tribes of Judah and Benjamin were loyal to Solomon's son, Rehoboam, but the ten northern tribes pledged their allegiance to one of Solomon's officials, Jeroboam.

Although the cycle of sin and repentance continued with both the Northern Kingdom, called Israel, and the Southern Kingdom, called Judah, the evil of idolatry reached its peak earlier in the north. For example, King Ahab built in Samaria a temple to the pagan god Baal. First Kings 16:33 states Ahab did more to provoke God to anger than did any of Israel's kings before him. His wife, Jezebel, is infamous for her killing spree of the Lord's prophets and her vow to kill Elijah after his showdown with the 450 false prophets of Baal on Mount Carmel. And this is only one example from two centuries of rebellion. The time came for God to reveal His holiness through judgment once again.

Historical Marker 2: 722 B.C.

Please read 2 Kings 17:5–15. How did God carry out His judgment against Israel, and what was the result?

List some of the reasons God brought judgment on Israel.

What actions did God take throughout Israel's history to protect the nation from judgment (vv. 12–15)?

The Northern Kingdom of Israel, with its ten tribes, was effectively brought to an end. Those Israelites were taken into captivity, and God never brought them back from exile. The few Israelites who were not removed from the land by the Assyrian king Sargon (721 B.C.) intermarried with the peoples the next Assyrian king, Esarhaddon (677 B.C.), brought in to settle there (2 Kings 17:24). Their descendants became the Samaritans.

Meanwhile back in the south, Judah continued the cycle of sin and repentance. King Josiah led Judah's final religious reform during his reign (640–609 B.C.). After Josiah's death, Judah had four consecutive kings whom the Bible describes as having done *"evil in the eyes of the LORD."* Together their reigns spanned 23 years (609–586 B.C.). These years were marked by constant oppression by other nations. Judah's kings responded to these nations alternately with submission and rebellion (2 Kings 23:31 through 24:20). God continued to warn Judah of His impending judgment, but the nation refused to repent. Finally, in 586 B.C., God brought judgment to Judah.

Historical Marker 3: 605 B.C.

Read Jeremiah 25:1–11. What message did God send to Judah through the prophet Jeremiah?

What reasons did God give for the coming judgment?

Historical Marker 4: 586 B.C.

Read 2 Kings 25:1–12. Describe the extent of God's judgment against Judah through the hands of Nebuchadnezzar, king of Babylon.

How was this event fulfillment of Jeremiah's prophecy?

The event described in 2 Kings 25 was the third and final exile of God's people from Judah to Babylon. Two previous exiles had taken place. In 605 B.C., the same year Nebuchadnezzar became king of Babylon, he gained control of the geographic area of Palestine, subjugating King Jehoiakim. He also took into captivity some of the best young men of Judah, including Daniel (Daniel 1:1–7 and 2 Chronicles 36:5–7). Eight years later, during the three-month reign of King Jehoiachin, Nebuchadnezzar and his armies returned to Jerusalem and took Judah's king and 10,000 inhabitants captive to Babylon (2 Kings 24:8–14).

In 586 B.C., after the fall of Jerusalem, things looked pretty bleak for God's chosen people. But human logic is often deceiving. Many times God had promised that He would spare a remnant and bring them back again. Both Isaiah and Jeremiah not only prophesied God's judgment on His people, but they also delivered God's message of restoration. (See Isaiah 10:20–21 and 11:11–12 and Jeremiah 23:3 and 31:7–8.)

Historical Marker 5: 538 B.C.

Read Ezra 1:1–11 and 3:1–3. List all the evidence you see of God's loving restoration in these two passages.

The way God used even a pagan king to fulfill His purposes is an example of His complete sovereignty. Can you think of times in your life when God carried out His will for you through unexpected ways?

About 150 years earlier, Isaiah prophesied this event, the return of the exiles. He even called Cyrus by name (Isaiah 44:24 through 45:1). Cyrus, the king of Persia, defeated Babylon in 539 B.C., taking over its territory and its captives. Just before the first exile in 605 B.C., Jeremiah not only prophesied that it would not be permanent, but he also specified the length of the exile to be 70 years (Jeremiah 25:8–11). (**Note:** One method of calculating the 70-year period is from the first captivity in 605 B.C. until the altar was rebuilt in Jerusalem in 536 B.C. [Ezra 3:1–3].)

These prophecies reveal that, even in judgment, God lovingly intended to protect and restore a remnant of His people. Even in discipline, God acts in love as a parent to a child (Hebrews 12:7–11). We cannot separate God's love from His justice. The Bible tells us God is holy, righteous, just, and loving. However, He does not act from justice alone in one situation and from love alone in another. He is one God, one nature. He is always just and always loving. It is from this unified nature that we see God relating to His people through the prophecy of Malachi.

     Can you recall a time when God acted in your life, revealing His unified nature? Describe what He revealed to you.

As we end today, thank God that He reveals His perfect holy nature to imperfect human beings.

DAY 2

God's Love Revealed by Malachi

Today we are finally getting to the Book of Malachi. The name *Malachi* literally means "my messenger" or "His messenger." Nothing is known about the author of this book of prophecy.

Although scholarly opinions vary about the *exact* date for authorship, educated guesses all fall within about a 30-year time frame. Because circumstances recorded in Malachi are similar to those in Ezra and Nehemiah, biblical scholars generally agree that Malachi was a prophet of God to Israel during the same period described in Ezra and Nehemiah. The following list of major events will help us understand the historical setting of Malachi.

538 B.C.	Edict by Cyrus, king of Persia, allowed the Israelites to return to Palestine to rebuild the Temple.
538 B.C.	First group of exiles returned under the leadership of Zerubbabel as governor and Joshua (also called Jeshua) as high priest.
536 B.C.	Rebuilding of the Temple began under Zerubbabel's leadership.
530 B.C.	Work on the Temple halted due to persecution from surrounding peoples.
520 B.C.	God spoke to His people through Haggai and Zechariah.
515 B.C.	Temple was completed through the encouragement of Haggai.
458 B.C.	Ezra returned to Jerusalem from Babylon with another group of exiles.

445 B.C. Nehemiah returned from Persia to Jerusalem to organize the rebuilding of the wall.

434 B.C. Nehemiah went back to Persia, but returned to Jerusalem after an unknown length of time.

We know from the text of Malachi that the Temple had already been rebuilt. Some scholars believe Malachi wrote while Ezra and Nehemiah served in Jerusalem. Others believe that Malachi was a prophet in Jerusalem during Nehemiah's return to Persia. This latter time frame is supported by the fact that Malachi has no mention of Ezra or Nehemiah, and the books of Ezra and Nehemiah don't mention him. Because the specific issues mentioned in Malachi are so similar to those in Nehemiah, it has been suggested that the dates for Malachi fall in the range of 445 B.C. to just after 434 B.C.

Although physically back in the land of Israel, the Jews were still subjects of the Persian Empire. Peoples of various heritages and religious practices surrounded them. Outwardly those Jews, the returned remnant, were serving Jehovah, God of Israel. They were conducting worship and offering sacrifices, but their lives and their hearts were not right before God. He had saved them and reestablished them in the Promised Land, but Israel did not respond properly to the love of a holy God. So, in love, God sent His messenger, Malachi, to call the people to repentance and restoration. The Book of Malachi is a picture of what happens in the lives of God's people when they do not fear Him.

Today we will become familiar with the Book of Malachi. It is important to read all of Malachi in one sitting. It is only four short chapters. Yet it is full of rich truths from God, which we will explore over the next few weeks. Its literary style is unique. As you read, notice the question-and-answer format. God posed questions through the prophet, and the people responded with their own questions.

Read through all of Malachi now. Don't read any study notes in your Bible. Let your first impression come from the Holy Spirit. What aspects of God's holy nature are revealed in the Book of Malachi?

Do you see any specific revelations of His love? If so, what are they?

Make a list below of the grievances God had with His people.

Do you see any similarities between the sins of Malachi's audience and God's people today? If so, what are they?

God desires to have a love relationship with us as He did with Israel. However, just as Israel did not respond properly to the love of a holy God, we often make the same mistakes.

Did the Holy Spirit bring anything specific to your attention today? Talk to God about it now.

DAY 3

Divine Love

Have you ever wondered if God *really* loves you? The Bible tells us again and again He does. Intellectually we may agree, but for various reasons, our hearts may question it. For instance, when the going gets tough, do we secretly wonder if God's love has run dry? When circumstances don't match our expectations, do we see that as a contradiction to God's declaration of love? I believe we also question God's love for us because we are using our experience with human love as a reference point.

My mother once told me about my father's first tentative declaration of love for her. It went something like this: "I *think* I love you." Her response was, "Well, when you get it figured out, let me know." Human love is not perfect. But God's love is never unsure, conditional, or selfish. And because God's holy nature is loving, He always *acts* in love toward us. The Book of Malachi, in fact, begins with a declaration of God's love for His people.

Read Malachi 1:1–2a. Why do you think the people questioned God's love for them?

Using what you learned about Israel's history with God in this week's day 1 study and your complete reading of Malachi, write a response to the people's question.

🖋 Have you ever questioned God's love for you? If yes, when and why?

Remember, God and His ways are infinitely above the ways of man. Our human minds cannot truly fathom the perfect love of God. Although God has revealed much in His Word about the nature of His love, this revelation falls short of its true greatness because, from necessity, God must describe His love in terms we can comprehend. This should not keep us, however, from attempting to explore and understand the depth of God's love for us. We can begin now and then experience it for all eternity. Let's take a closer look at what the Bible has to say about the nature of God's love. Numerous adjectives and descriptive phrases are used to help us understand the divine affection.

Read through the Scripture passages in table 3. Use the table to compile some facts about God's love. Note each adjective or descriptive phrase used to describe the love of God. Some passages have multiple ideas, so watch for those. Record any insights you gain by considering why a certain descriptive phrase was used. I have begun the first one to get you started. Keep in mind this is merely the tip of the iceberg. Continue to allow God to teach you about His love for you. (*Note:* Depending on the translation you are using, you may see the words *mercy* or *kindness* used synonymously with *love*.)

Table 3. Nature of God's love

SCRIPTURE	DESCRIPTIVE WORDS OR PHRASES	PERSONAL INSIGHT
Psalm 32:10	*Unfailing; leads us; surrounds those who trust*	*God's love is completely dependable; it surrounds me in protection and for comfort and affection*

Table 1 is continued on next page.

Psalm 36:5		
Psalm 63:3		
Psalm 94:18		
2 Corinthians 5:14		
1 John 3:1		

I am overwhelmed at the thought that a holy God loves the likes of me. Praise God! His love for us is not because we merit it, but because, in His grace, He has chosen to love us. And this love is not the flawed love we receive from other humans; it is perfect and divine love.

If you have ever questioned God's love, reflect on the passages in table 3 to allow God to solidly confirm His love for you!

As we end today, express your awe and thankfulness to God for His love. If you wish, you may record your prayer of thankfulness to God in the following space.

DAY 4

Holy Love

Time and again God showed His love for Israel through His saving acts. He took Joseph and then Joseph's family to Egypt to preserve them through a severe famine (Genesis 50:20). Through God's miracles and the leadership of Moses and Joshua, God brought the Israelites out of slavery in Egypt, through 40 years in the desert, and into the Promised Land. God raised up numerous judges and kings to save Israel from one enemy nation after another. God sent prophets to call His people to repentance so they could be saved from the judgment their sin deserved. And when they did not repent and judgment came, God saved a remnant of His chosen people so He could restore the nation. This is Malachi's audience.

The primary way God reveals His love to us is as He did to Israel: He does it through salvation. But remember, even in salvation, God does not act merely from love if it means compromising another aspect of His character. For instance, God does not simply sweep our sin under the rug so He can lovingly save us. This scenario of salvation is impossible because it would cause God to act unjustly. Although we may be aware of one divine characteristic more than the others in an encounter with God, every one of His acts is an expression of the entirety of who He is.

When I, as a child, was disobedient and about to experience parental discipline, my mom or dad would often say, "I'm doing this because I love you." I thought, "Yeah, right."

When I was about six years old, I picked a lovely tiger lily out of our neighbors' yard. I knew it didn't belong to me, but it was pretty, and I wanted it. When I presented the lily to my mother, she made me march, with flower in hand, right over to the neighbors' house, knock on their front door, and tell them what I had done.

Now that I'm a parent, I can understand the loving purpose behind my mother's discipline. I needed to learn respect for others' property. I needed to learn to take responsibility for my actions. And I have to say that I've used the same technique on my own children because it made an impact on me.

Today I recognize my mother's love in that situation, but all I remember feeling at the time is my mother's displeasure. Although this is an imperfect human example, it does illustrate the fact that while at times, we may sense only one aspect of God's character, He always acts in complete accordance with everything He is. In *The Holiness of God*, R. C. Sproul puts it this way: "What God *does* is always consistent with who God *is*. He always acts according to His holy character."[1] The following passages will help us understand how this truth works in our salvation through Christ's death.

Please read the following passages, and record what aspect or quality of God's character or nature is being revealed. You may

want to read them from more than one translation to capture a broader sense of the meaning. (***Note:*** Some passages may reveal more than one facet of God's nature.)

- **John 3:16**
- **Romans 5:8**
- **Ephesians 2:4–5**
- **1 John 4:9–10**
- **Romans 3:22–26**

After reading these passages, explain how God reveals His entire nature in the act of our salvation.

The unity of God's nature is displayed in the act of salvation. I know I have been guilty of focusing on God's love when I consider my salvation, while ignoring the cost that God's justice demanded. Oswald Chambers elaborates:

> The great miracle of the grace of God is that He forgives sin, and it is the death of Jesus Christ alone that enables the divine nature to forgive and to remain true to itself in doing so. It is shallow nonsense to say that God forgives us because He is love. Once we have been convicted of sin, we will never say this again. The love of God means Calvary— nothing less! The love of God is spelled out on the Cross and nowhere else. The only basis on which God can forgive me is the Cross of Christ. It is there that His conscience is satisfied.[2]
> —Oswald Chambers, *My Utmost for His Highest*

Scripture is clear that God loves us and desires to have a relationship with us. But our sin separates us from a holy God. This conflict could be reconciled only in the Cross. God's love was the motivation, and His justice was the method. As we will see repeatedly, whatever God demands from us, He also provides. He demanded the death penalty for our sin and then provided it Himself through the death of Christ.

Have you personally experienced God's great salvation? Because every one of us has sinned by choosing our own way over God's perfect way (Romans 3:12), we all deserve the death penalty (Romans 6:23). God's forgiveness is possible because Christ willingly gave His own life on the Cross to pay the penalty our sin earned. If there has never been a point in time when you made the decision to receive God's forgiveness and the eternal life it brings, if you have never given your life to God and received Jesus as your Lord and Savior, why not do that right now? If you aren't sure how to do this, talk with your Bible study leader.

The Apostle Paul beautifully expressed in a prayer his desire for the believers in Ephesus to be able to grasp the enormity of God's love:

> *And I pray that you, being rooted and established in love, may have power, together with all the saints, to grasp how wide and long and high and deep is the love of Christ, and to know this love that surpasses knowledge—that you may be filled to the measure of all the fullness of God.*
>
> —Ephesians 3:17–19

✒ As we end today, write your own prayer in the space below, asking God to reveal to you His enormous love.

Day 5

Chosen in Love

My family and I recently moved from Alberta, Canada, to Texas. To find a house, my husband and I visited our new city a couple of months before the move. After a few days of hunting, we had narrowed the field to two houses, but we were having trouble choosing between them. So we made a list. We gave the two houses names to keep them straight. One house we called "the Kentucky Derby house" because one day when we viewed it, the residents were watching the Kentucky Derby. The other house we called "Bob"; I really don't remember why.

Our pros and cons list included items like size, condition, layout, and location. My husband favored one because of the larger garage. I favored the other because of the larger kitchen. In the end, Bob and the bigger kitchen won out. We had made our choice based on the merits of the house and how it would serve our family.

What generally drives your decision-making process?

Read Malachi 1:1–5 and Romans 9:10–18; then compare the two passages. God made a choice, as revealed in Malachi 1:1–3. What was it?

Based on the additional information given in the Romans passage, on what basis did God make this choice?

God does not make choices in the same way we do. Not only are His thinking and ways infinitely higher than ours, but also He has the ultimate *right* to choose. This is true in everything, including to whom God chooses to give eternal life. R. C. Sproul comments on this:

> We soon forget that with our first sin we have forfeited all rights to the gift of life. That I am drawing breath this morning is an act of divine mercy. God owes me nothing. I owe Him everything.... We think we deserve more grace.... It is impossible for anyone, anywhere, anytime to *deserve* grace. Grace by definition is undeserved.[3]
>
> —R. C. Sproul, *The Holiness of God*

If God has the right to choose who will receive mercy, does this mean that some people have no chance of salvation? Did Esau ever have a chance? Before we answer this question, let's take a look at some other passages. We don't want to make the mistake of basing doctrine on isolated passages. We want to consider everything in the light of the totality of God's Word.

Read 1 Timothy 2:3–6. What does this passage teach us about the scope of God's salvation?

God chose Jacob over his brother, Esau, to be the father of the nation of Israel. God set this nation apart as His people and declared them holy in order that they would reveal Him to the world. Therefore, God's ultimate purpose in choosing Jacob over Esau was the salvation of all mankind.

Many of you are probably familiar with the story of the twin brothers, Jacob and Esau, in the Book of Genesis. Remember that Esau was born a few minutes before Jacob. Therefore, as the firstborn, he had the right to a double portion of the family inheritance and the special blessing of his father, Isaac. However, an incident recorded in Genesis 25 put a kink in this tradition. It also revealed a lot about both Jacob and Esau.

Read Genesis 25:27–34 and Hebrews 12:14–17, and compare the two passages. Based on these two passages, write a character sketch of Esau. Specifically look for attitudes and actions that reveal his heart condition toward God.

Because God is all knowing, He thoroughly knows the heart of every person. While Jacob was far from perfect (as shown in this story of him taking advantage of his brother's hunger), Esau had a dangerous attitude that had deep roots in his heart. The writer of Hebrews calls him *"godless"* (12:16). Esau rejected God and His ways. He had a casual attitude toward God and eternal things. This attitude was demonstrated when he traded his birthright for a meal. Esau traded something that was still in the future, yet held lasting value, for something that was immediate, yet fleeting.

Look again at Hebrews 12:14. The writer of Hebrews emphasized the necessity of holiness in the lives of believers. In fact, he went on to use Esau as a negative example. Christians, those to whom God gives His great gift of salvation, are to live holy lives. They are not to act like Esau. God, in His omniscience and sovereignty, chose Jacob over Esau to be the father of a nation. And again in His omniscience and sovereignty, God chose you to receive eternal salvation through Jesus Christ. Let's take a closer look at this *choosing*.

Read Ephesians 1:3–6. Why did God choose you? When did God choose you? How did God choose you? And for what purpose did God choose you?

Chose in Ephesians 1:4 is translated from the Greek word *eklegomai*. *Strong's Greek and Hebrew Dictionary* includes in its definition the phrase *"to choose out for one's self."*[4] Fellow believer, I hope the thought that God picked you out lovingly for Himself forever leaves a mark on your heart. Before He even created the world, God looked forward in time, settled His gaze on you, and said, "This one is Mine."

Take a moment to write a prayer of gratitude to God for having chosen you.

Now let's turn our attention to God's *purpose* in choosing. Ephesians 1:4 states that God chose us to be *"holy and blameless."* The Bible repeatedly tells us we are to be holy because God is holy (for example, Leviticus 11:44–45 and 1 Peter 1:14–16). Mankind was created in the image of God, designed to be in relationship with Him and to reflect His glory to all of creation. But sin in humans distorted the reflected image of God and broke the relationship, bringing death.

Yet, in love, God made it possible for individuals to be redeemed from death and restored into a relationship with Him. Then through this relationship, God calls us to live holy lives, reflecting His glory to a lost world. Because God is holy, He calls His people to be holy. Recall our discussion on the holiness of God from week 1, day 4. God's holiness means He is separate from all that is sinful and profane. This, then, is our calling as believers: to separate ourselves from all that is sinful and profane.

First Samuel 2:2 states, *"There is no one holy like the LORD."* God calls us to be holy; to live lives separated from the sin and ungodliness of this world. And we must strive to do just that through the power of His Holy Spirit. But we will never attain God's level of holiness. His holiness is infinite because He is God. We are not.

So what should holiness look like in our lives? According to John 15:19, Jesus told His followers that He had chosen them *"out of the world."* The Bible often uses the term *world* to signify all that is ungodly or unholy. In the surrounding Scriptures, Jesus described the life of one who has been called *"out of the world"* and, instead, remains in His love.

Read John 15:9–21, 26–27. As you read these verses, make a list below of traits and characteristics that should be evident in the life of one who has been chosen.

As we end today, let's examine our own lives. First, ask God to reveal any attitudes of your heart that are similar to Esau's. Next, ask Him to show you characteristics that should be strongly evident in the life of a chosen one but are weak in your life. Finally, confess, repent, and ask God to make you holy so you can reflect His glory to a lost world.

WEEK 3

GOD DESCRIBES A "FEARLESS" LIFE

Are you still with me? Our busy lives often derail us in our commitment to an in-depth Bible study. We get a little behind, and then a lot behind, and then we quit. If you are already behind, don't be discouraged. And don't get bogged down trying to catch up. Just start fresh from right here. In fact, I think this would be a good time for a recap.

In the week 1 study, "God Deserves Our Fear," we explored the biblical basis for godly fear. Not only does the Bible present the fear of God as a positive and desirable attitude, it depicts it as the only *proper* attitude we should have toward the one true and holy God. We also took a closer look at the holy nature of God, which inspires our fear.

In week 2, we saw that God reveals His divine love to those who fear Him. We reviewed the history of the nation of Israel to set the stage for the Book of Malachi. We witnessed God's love for His chosen nation through that history. Because the Book of Malachi begins with a declaration of love from God, we briefly explored through Scriptures the nature of His love and what it means to us. We also discussed how His love works together with all the other aspects of His holy nature. We ended the week by emphasizing the truth that because God is holy, He has chosen us to be holy.

In love, God chose us to be His. He wants us to live holy lives with an attitude of godly fear. You may still be wondering what that looks like. I often find it helpful to understand what something *is* by pointing out what it *is not*. God does the same thing in the Book of Malachi. The list you made on day 2 of week 2 regarding grievances God had with Malachi's audience is evidence that the people did not fear God. This week, we will take a closer look at a few of those "fearless" attitudes.

DAY 1

Son or Servant? Yes to Both

Christians today often use God's role as our Father to minimize what it means to fear Him. It is true that if we have received Christ's gift of salvation, God has adopted us as His child. However, we often have the wrong idea, especially in today's culture, about how a child should respond to a parent. And our heavenly Father is not just your run-of-the-mill, ball-throwing, everyday dad. He is a holy God. He is also our Lord and Master. And we often treat Him too casually.

How would you act if you met the President of the United States? I would probably stammer and stutter while I tried to decide if I should curtsey or bow. Although it is a weak human example, we can compare our potential response to the President with our real response to God. The President, although he is an imperfect human being, is given respect because of who he is. While he is an elected official and a servant of the people, he is also the commander in chief of one of the most powerful nations in the world. His position generates simultaneous responses of thankfulness, friendship, loyalty, awe, respect, and maybe even a little fear. Most of us would never dream of calling the President by his first name (to his face, anyway) or of putting our feet up on the coffee table in the Oval Office. And we would never hand him a list titled, "Things I Need You to Do for Me." We would never dare to be that casual or demanding with a man in his position.

How does that compare with your response to Jehovah's position as the one true and holy God, Creator of all that is? Should we respond to Him as Father or as Master? The answer is yes. Today we will see that the Bible uses both son and slave to describe the nature of our relationship to God.

Read Malachi 1:6. Based on this verse, what type of relationship did God expect to have with the priests?

What attitudes should be demonstrated in this relationship?

Language Notes

Malachi 1:6

English: **honor**
Hebrew: *kabed*
Definition: to be heavy, be weighty, be grievous, be hard, be rich, be honorable, be glorious, be burdensome, be honored

God is addressing the priests in Malachi 1:6. The religious leaders, the ones who were set aside as God's representatives and faithful examples to the people, were failing to give God the honor and fear He deserved. Apparently they were honoring their earthly fathers, but not their heavenly Father. Matthew Henry, in his commentary on the Bible, said, "Our relation to God as our Father and Master strongly obliges us to fear and honour him. If we honour and fear the fathers of our flesh, much more the Father and Master of our spirits."[1] I am afraid many Christians in America today would show more respect in a meeting with the President than in meeting with God in worship or prayer.

> **How often do you contemplate the high and exalted position of our Lord? How might considering this reality affect the attitude you take before Him?**

Let's get a better handle on what Malachi 1:6 should mean to us today by taking a look at what it meant to the original audience. Our contemporary society views both the father-child relationship and the master-slave relationship quite differently than did Malachi's audience.

Let's examine the father-child relationship first by considering the meaning of the original Hebrew word for "honor," as shown in the language notes on page 42. *Kabed* implies figurative heaviness or weight. A person who "carries a lot of weight" is someone who is honorable, impressive, and worthy of respect.[2]

The father in Israel's ancient patriarchal system was a person who was worthy of *kabed* (honor). According to *Manners and Customs of Bible Lands* by Fred Wight, the father had supreme authority over all in his household. The children demonstrated a high level of reverence, respect, and obedience to their fathers.[3] The father was the center of ancient family life.[4] Over and over, God's Word makes it clear that children were (and are) to honor their fathers. It was expected in biblical times and continues to be God's standard today. Unfortunately, that standard has slipped in some of today's societies. Many children don't even know *how* to honor their fathers.

Review the original meaning of the Hebrew word for "honor" in light of the cultural information. Does this biblical father-child relationship differ from that in today's culture? How?

In what way, if any, does this insight change your perception of God as your Father?

Now let's turn to the nature of the master-slave relationship. Slavery in ancient Israel was very different from that seen in the history of the United States. Although some slaves were abused, the master-slave relationship was often an arrangement that benefited both master and slave. Individuals who were down on their luck would often sell themselves into slavery to survive. Because of the provision of the master, the life of a slave was usually better than the life of a free peasant. Slaves were considered property, but they were not without rights. There were laws to protect them, and they could even earn their freedom. (**Note:** In Malachi 1:6, the attitude that a slave should display to his master is the Hebrew word *mora'*. It is translated as "respect" in some translations and as "fear" in others. *Mora'* comes from the root word *yare'*, which we defined in week 1, day 3.)

How does the idea of slavery apply to our relationship with God? The Apostle Paul wrote, *"Do you not know that your body is a temple of the Holy Spirit, who is in you, whom you have received from God? You are not your own; you were bought at a price. Therefore honor God with your body"* (1 Corinthians 6:19–20). Before you were a Christian, you were a slave to sin. But God, in His mercy, redeemed you from slavery to wickedness so that you might become slaves to righteousness (Romans 6:17–22). The price was the blood of Christ. When God redeemed you, He placed the Holy Spirit within you as His mark of ownership. If you are a Christian, you do not belong to yourself; you have no rights of your own. You belong to God. He has the right of ownership and authority over your life.

How do you feel about the idea of God as Owner and Master of your life? Do you see this as a negative or positive concept and why?

In Malachi 1:6, God declares Himself as both Father and Master, which makes us both child and slave. Although initially this comparison may seem contradictory, we need both analogies to properly understand the nature of our relationship with God. When these are viewed together, a tension is created between God as Master and God as Father that helps us better understand what it means to fear God. A proper balance will keep us from either treating God too casually or remaining too distant. Jerry Bridges elaborates in his book *The Joy of Fearing God:*

> There should always be a healthy tension between the confidence with which we come before God as His children and the reverential awe with which we behold Him as our sovereign Lord.... We have indeed received the Spirit of adoption.... He is still the King who is eternal, immortal, and invisible, and who lives in unapproachable light.[5]
>
> —Jerry Bridges, *The Joy of Fearing God*

Describe a relationship with God that views Him only as Father. Include both positive and negative aspects.

Describe a relationship with God that views Him only as Master. Include both positive and negative aspects.

New Testament authors make use of both the father-child and master-slave analogies. When the whole of the Scriptures is considered and individual passages understood in light of other passages, we get a clearer picture of our standing as both free child and slave.

Read Romans 6:16–18, 22–23. What things held us in slavery before we were saved?

What is the result of slavery to sin?

What is the result of slavery to God and righteousness?

> **Language**
>
> **1 Peter 2:16**
>
> English: **free/freedom**
> Greek: *eleutheros*
> Definition: refers to one who is not a slave; one who ceases to be a slave, freed; unrestrained, not bound by obligation
>
> English: **slave**
> Greek: *doulos*
> Definition: refers to one who is a slave, bondman, man of servile condition; one who gives himself up to another's will; devoted to another to the disregard of one's own interests

Read Romans 8:12–17. According to this passage, what benefits do we have as God's children?

What do you think the phrase *"slave again to fear"* (v. 15) means based on the context of this passage?

If you are a Christian, you are free! You are free from obligation to the law, free from the control of sin, and free from the fear of judgment. Adopted by God, you have all the rights of heirs. Your adoption came at a great price. The purchase price of your redemption was the life of Christ. God *bought* you out of slavery to sin and the law. You are not your own; you belong to Him.

Peter wrote, *"You are not slaves; you are free. But your freedom is not an excuse to do evil. You are free to live as God's slaves"* (1 Peter 2:16 NLT). Please refer to the language notes on previous page for insight from the original language. You were freed from slavery so you would be free to submit yourself as a slave to God! Yet you are a slave of God with all the rights and privileges of an heir.

Jerry Bridges describes the tension created by these two ideas as opposing forces. The fatherly love of God is the "centripetal force" that draws us close to Him. The tension is created, he says, when other of God's attributes, such as His justice and sovereignty—the "centrifugal force"—keep us at a reverent distance. He concludes, "To exercise a proper fear of God we must understand and respond to both these forces."[6] Our adoption allows us complete access to the Father. God's status as Master should foster a "fearful" attitude that completely yields to His authority over our lives.

☙ **Prayerfully consider where your attitude before God would fall on the spectrum below, and mark that spot with an X.**

Child _____ Slave

☙ **Does your relationship with God reveal a proper balance between child and slave?   Yes   No   (Circle one.)**

☙ **Are you too casual or too distant with God?**

 As we close today, respond to what God has revealed to you that needs adjustment in your relationship with Him.

DAY 2

Fear Deficit

Not long ago, one of my teenage children was munching on some candy. It sounded really good, so even though I was, as usual, trying to carefully watch what I was eating, I asked if I could have a little bit.

"Oh sure, Mom," was the reply. "You can have *all* the green ones! I don't really like that color very much; plus some of them fell on the floor."

Extremely sacrificial of her, don't you think? I am sure that offer came straight from a heart of love and devotion. We may shake our heads in frustration or even laugh at these kinds of attitudes from our kids, but how do you think God views it when we offer Him "all the green ones"?

Malachi 1:6–14 focuses on the nature of the sacrifices the people were bringing to God and the disastrous results. We will camp on this section of the book for the rest of the week, highlighting a different aspect each day.

Read Malachi 1:6–14. Describe the condition of the people's sacrifices. (***Note:*** See language notes for a definition of *defiled*. In addition, the *Theological Wordbook of the Old Testament* describes *ga'al* [defilement] as a "breach of moral or ceremonial law.")[7]

Hold your place in Malachi. Let's take a quick detour to Leviticus to learn about God's expectations for the sacrificial animals. We don't need to go into the different types of sacrifices and when and how they were used, but watch for the requirements for the *condition* of the sacrificial animals.

Language Notes

Malachi 1:6

English: **fear/reverence/awe**
Hebrew: *mora'* (from the root *yare'*)
Definition: fear, reverence, terror

Malachi 1:14

English: **fear/reverence/awe**
Hebrew: *yare'*
Definition: to fear, be afraid; to stand in awe of, be awed; to fear, reverence, honor, respect

Read Leviticus 22:17–25. Describe the expectations God had for a sacrificial animal.

Why do you think God set such high standards?

Refer back to Malachi 1:6–14. How well did the people's sacrifices measure up to God's requirements?

Describe God's response to sacrifices that were less than He demanded.

Why in the world would the people offer as sacrifices to God animals that so obviously did not meet His commanded standards? What were they thinking when they went to the corral to pick out their animals? I picture the people described in Malachi thinking something like this: "Let's see.... Maybe I should take Handsome Hank over there. Hmmm.... Well, he's really a ladies' man. If I take him, it might affect how many calves I have in the spring. OK, how about Strong Steve? No, I'm really going to need him come planting time. I know! I'll choose Weak Wade. That bull couldn't fight his way out of a papyrus sack if his life depended on it. Yep. I'll offer Wade to God. He isn't much use to me anyway."

What do you see in Malachi 1:6–14 that explains why the people chose to offer defiled sacrifices?

The first and last verses of this passage (vv. 6 and 14) reveal the heart attitudes that were present in the offering of defiled sacrifices. (See language notes on previous page.) God's priests did not honor or fear Him, and it showed in their actions. If the priests of Malachi's day had feared

> **Language Notes**
>
> **Malachi 1:7, 12**
> English: **defiled**
> Hebrew: *ga'al*
> Definition: to defile, pollute, or desecrate

God, He would have been pleased with both their sacrifices and their lives. Moses gave a good description of a "fearful" life that pleases God:

"And now, Israel, what does the LORD your God require of you? He requires you to fear him, to live according to his will, to love and worship him with all your heart and soul, and to obey the LORD's commands and laws that I am giving you today for your own good."

—Deuteronomy 10:12–13 (NLT)

Based on this passage (Deuteronomy 10:12–13), write a description of a person who fears God. (***Note:*** Five verbs in this passage answer the question, What does the Lord require of you? The first one is *yare'*, our Hebrew word for "fear.")

✒ **As we end today, ask God to evaluate your life in light of Deuteronomy 10:12–13. Write a prayer of response.**

DAY 3

Condition of the Sacrifice

According to the November 3, 2003, article by The Barna Group, 84 percent of American adults consider themselves to be Christian. Yet statistics reveal a significant conflict between what Americans consider to be morally acceptable behavior and the moral teachings of the Christian faith. For instance, gambling is considered to be morally acceptable by 61 percent of those polled; abortion, 45 percent; cohabitation, 60 percent; adultery, 42 percent; looking at pornography, 38 percent; getting drunk, 35 percent; and homosexual behavior, 30 percent.[8]

Despite America's casual attitude regarding sin, we have made a special claim on God and His blessings. Our banner cry since September 11, 2001, seems to be "God bless America!" We live as slaves to the world and its ways instead of slaves to righteousness, yet we hold out our hands and boldly ask for God's blessings. Is it because we know that God is gracious, and we plan to take full advantage of it? *"What shall we say, then?"* wrote the Apostle Paul. *"Shall we go on sinning so that grace may increase?"*

(Romans 6:1). Jerry Bridges, in *The Joy of Fearing God*, states that people who stubbornly continue to live in sin, claiming the hope of God's grace, apparently have no fear of God and His discipline. "Anytime we sin with the thought lurking in the back of our minds that God will forgive us, we aren't living in the fear of God."[9]

Read Malachi 1:8–11. In verse 9, what did the people dare expect from God after they brought their sacrifice?

What was God's response?

Now it is time to make this personal. How can we apply the concept of defiled sacrifices to our own lives? The sacrificial death of Christ was the final, perfect sacrifice (Hebrews 10:11–14). His offering completely did away with the need for animal sacrifices. So does God require a sacrifice from Christians today? Yes!

> *And so, dear brothers and sisters, I plead with you to give your bodies to God. Let them be a living and holy sacrifice—the kind he will accept. When you think of what he has done for you, is this too much to ask? Don't copy the behavior and customs of this world, but let God transform you into a new person by changing the way you think. Then you will know what God wants you to do, and you will know how good and pleasing and perfect his will really is.*
>
> —Romans 12:1–2 (NLT)

What is the sacrifice God wants?

The *"sacrifice"* referred to in Romans 12:1 is not an offering to atone for sin. Only the perfect sacrifice of Christ could take care of our sin. Rather, this Romans 12:1 sacrifice is a thank offering.

The urging of Paul to his readers—then and now—is to respond to the saving mercy and grace of God, which Paul presented in the first part of Romans. Since God has freed us from the death of sin, our proper response is to willingly and completely offer Him our new lives.

So what should be the condition of our sacrifice? Does the Bible give any directives for this new *living sacrifice* like those given for the animal sacrifices of the Old Covenant? Romans 12:1 indicates our sacrifice, or our very life, will be pleasing to God if it is holy. Do you remember the explanation on day 4 of week 1 about *qadosh*, the Hebrew word for "holy"? *Qadosh* refers to that which is separate from all that is sinful and profane. The lives of Christians are to be *qadosh*.

Colossians 3 reveals the contrasts between unholy behavior and the lifestyle that pleases God. Read Colossians 3:1–17, and fill in table 4.

Table 4. Worldly versus transformed behavior

WORLDLY/UNHOLY BEHAVIOR	TRANSFORMED/HOLY BEHAVIOR

✒ Ask God to reveal to you the condition of your sacrifice. Does your life reflect any behavior you listed on the left side of table 4?

🐚 **Are any of the attitudes or behaviors on the right side of table 4 absent from your life?**

Remember, none of us will be perfected this side of heaven. Our time on earth is a process of growing to be more and more like Christ. But, praise God, *"The sacrifices of God are a broken spirit; a broken and contrite heart, O God, you will not despise"* (Psalm 51:17). Hearts broken before the Lord are accessible to Him and open to His touch. Will you allow Him full access?

DAY 4

The Dishonoring of God's Name

What's in a name? That which we call a rose / By any other name would smell as sweet." This quote from William Shakespeare's play *Romeo and Juliet* reveals that the character Juliet didn't seem to put much stock in a name. Maybe that handsome Romeo just kept her from thinking straight. Consider the infamous moniker *Jezebel*. Would you ever consider naming one of your children after that cruel queen of Israel? Today the name is used as a descriptive term for someone who is scheming and evil. Think about the name *Benedict Arnold*. The name of this traitorous American general of the Revolutionary War will always be synonymous with betrayal. On the other hand, the name *Florence Nightingale* provides a positive example of how names tend to become significant. The tireless service of this nineteenth-century English nurse ensured that her name would become a symbol for dedication, commitment, and selflessness.

Based on Malachi 1:6–14, Jehovah seemed to be very concerned about how His name was treated. Today we will explore the significance of God's name and consider its relevance for us.

Read again Malachi 1:6–14. Note all the references to God's name in this passage. Describe the difference between how the priests of Israel treated God's name and how the nations (Gentiles) will one day treat it. (*Note: Yare'*, our Hebrew word for "fear," is found in verse 14.)

The Ten Commandments can be found in Exodus 20:1–17. Based on what we found in Malachi, postexilic Israel didn't do such a great job of keeping the third commandment (v. 7). Let's take a moment to focus on this divine directive. It will not only help us better understand our passage in Malachi, but also provide some meaningful truths we can apply to our own lives.

> *Thou shalt not take the name of the LORD thy God in vain; for the LORD will not hold him guiltless that taketh his name in vain.*
>
> —Exodus 20:7 (KJV)

The same Hebrew word is translated as "name" in both the first chapter of Malachi and in Exodus 20:7. *Name* or *mark* implies the honor, authority, and character of its bearer. Names were significant in the ancient world. People believed they summed up the essence or character of an individual. God's name is synonymous with who He is. God's name is representative of His holy nature. Therefore, whatever we do to the divine name, we also do to God Himself. If we bring honor to the name of God, we bring honor to God. If we take His name lightly, we are taking God Himself lightly. God has told us not to take His name in vain. But what does that mean?

Review the language notes. Considering the original language and the meaning of names in ancient times, do you have any new insight on the third commandment? If so, what is it?

Does this new insight broaden your understanding of Malachi 1:6–14? If so, in what ways?

Read 1 Timothy 6:1 for a New Testament application. Although this example concerns the behavior of Christian slaves with their

---

Language Notes

Exodus 20:7

English: **name/mark**
Hebrew: *shem* (also in Malachi 1:6–14)
Definition: mark or memorial of individuality

English: **vain**
Hebrew: *shaw'*
Definition: emptiness, nothingness, or vanity, in the sense of being ineffective or lacking in purpose

English: **take**
Hebrew: *nasa'*
Definition: lift, lift up, to bear, carry, support, sustain (can be literal or figurative)

masters, what principle is found in this passage that should be applied to Christians today?

If we bear the name *Christian,* everything we do has an impact on the name of Christ. Although I know this is true, I sometimes act in the moment without considering the effects my behavior will have on the kingdom. One day I was on my way to church to lead a ladies' Tuesday-morning Bible study class. I was running late. Two stoplights from my destination, the driver of the only car in front of me sat through the green light without making a move while she talked to the person in the passenger seat. I "patiently" waited behind her until the next green light.

When the light changed to green again, it looked as if she might not make that one either, so I blasted my horn. No, it was not a friendly, quick toot. It was an irritated, long blast. She began to move and slowly made it through the intersection. As soon as I had the chance, I darted around her, tossing back one of those icy glares as I sped by. I approached the last light and got in the right lane to make my turn. I glanced in my rearview mirror. She was also in the right turn lane. One block from church, I was hit with a horrible possibility. What if the woman in the car was headed to my church? A community group meets in our building on Tuesday mornings. She would see me go in and know I was one of those "Christian" women. "No," I reassured myself. "What are the chances? Surely she is headed to one of the homes in the neighborhood."

I slowed to make the turn into the church parking lot. Another furtive glance in the mirror confirmed my worst fears. She was also turning! I scooted into the one remaining parking spot close to the doors, while she drove further down the lot. I quickly went inside the building and headed to my classroom before she got her seat belt unfastened. My only consolation was that even though she could identify my car, she might not have gotten a good look at my face. Recognizing my behavior as sin, I immediately prayed that my actions would not have a negative spiritual impact on that woman. As a Christian, I am God's representative. My every action and attitude shape God's reputation before a lost world.

Consider the fact that Christians take or bear God's name. List some examples of how Christians today take the name of God in vain. Remember to apply what we just learned. This area is much broader than our speech.

🕊 **As we end today, prayerfully ask God to reveal to you any way you may have misused or borne His name too casually. Ask Him to give you a constant awareness of the way you represent Him to a watching world.**

Day 5

Sacrifices God Accepts

This is our last day on the first chapter of Malachi. We may not have traveled far this week, but we have dug deep into some important issues. Today we will review what we have learned this week so we can make some personal application.

On day 1, we considered this question: Are we son or slave? As we saw from Scriptures, the answer is that we are both God's child and slave. In fact, understanding the tension between the two analogies helps us to understand what it means to properly fear God. Consider this tension in light of your own life.

🕊 **Have you been too casual with God, forgetting that He is holy? If so, how?**

🕊 **Have you taken advantage of your position as God's child, merely bringing Him lists of requests you would like for Him to fulfill?**

On days 2 and 3, we discovered that defiled lives reveal a lack of godly fear. As Christians, our very lives are the sacrifices that God desires. But God does not accept defiled or impure sacrifices. Sacrifices that are pure and holy are the ones that are pleasing to Him.

🕊 **Are you giving God the best of your time, resources, and talents, or are you giving Him the "green ones," the leftovers, the things you don't want?**

🕊 Review table 4 (in this week's day 3 study), which compares worldly/unholy and transformed/holy behavior. Did God reveal any more behaviors and attitudes in your life that do not please Him?

Read and meditate on Psalm 51:1–17.

🕊 Does this prayer of confession, repentance, and restoration speak to any current issues in your life? If so, spend time in prayer now. Ask God to cleanse you, making your life holy and pleasing as an offering to Him.

On day 4, we found that defiled offerings bring dishonor to the name of God. We explored the meaning of the third commandment and applied it to the lives of Christians today.

Read the following passages. Describe the kind of offering or sacrifice that God desires.
- 1 Samuel 15:22
- Hosea 6:6
- Micah 6:6–8
- Mark 12:28–34

🕊 What are some ways that you can bring honor to God's name through the sacrifice of your life?

In our study this week, we saw that God's priests offered defiled sacrifices because they did not fear Him. For Christians, because our very lives are the sacrifices that God desires, the way we live reveals whether we truly fear Him.

🕊 What does your life reveal? Do your attitude and level of obedience show that you fear God?

🕊 Rate yourself on a scale of 1 to 10, with 10 being a full measure of godly fear. What areas still need work?

How are you doing? God is certainly using the truths brought out in His Word to do a work in my own life. His desire is to conform us to the image of His Son.

As we end this week, let's thank Him for what He wants to do in each of our lives.

WEEK 4

GOD'S COVENANT DEMANDS FEAR

I could make a long list of well-known leaders who have "fallen from grace" in my lifetime. My list would include politicians, athletes, actors, and—sadly—religious leaders. When a leader falls, the results can be disastrous. Persons who have respected and followed that leader may feel disillusioned, betrayed, angry, or even hopeless. However, there is something worse than a leader who falls out of favor with his or her followers and is rejected: it's a leader who uses his or her powerful influence to guide people down a wrong or even dangerous path. This situation is what we find in Malachi.

God was not pleased with the priests, as we saw in the first chapter of Malachi. They showed no honor or fear for God as their Father and Master. The evidence God cited was their willingness to offer defiled sacrifices on the altar for themselves and the people. As we now move into chapter 2 of Malachi, we see that God elaborated on the severity and scope of this situation. God had chosen and established a covenant with the tribe of Levi to serve Him and be the spiritual leaders of God's people. The priests were Levites who were descendants of Aaron. God chose them from among the Levites for special service. God charged the Levites, specifically the priests, with breaking His covenant of leadership. As go the leaders, so go the followers.

DAY 1

Fear Required in Levitical Covenant

It is a lot easier to start well than to finish well. I have many half-finished projects lying around my house. For example, a hooked rug with a sea-shell pattern, which I started in high school, remains incomplete. I haven't touched it since 1975. Then there is the barely begun cross-stitch picture I started for my husband in 1987. I also have vacation scrapbooks that record only part of the trip, half-read books, and half-written letters. The list goes on.

In God's grand scheme of life, these things are insignificant. However, some tasks are God-given tasks that He intends to use for His purposes. In the second chapter of Malachi, we will consider the task of leadership that God gave to the Levites. We will see later this week that the Levites did not remain faithful in their role; they did not remain faithful to their God-given task. However, today we will focus on their good beginning.

Let's jump back to about a millennium before the time of Malachi and read the original account of God's covenant with the tribe of Levi. This will give us the proper background we need to better understand what is happening in Malachi.

Read Numbers 8:5–19. Describe the elements of the Levites' dedication ceremony and why you think they are significant.

Read Deuteronomy 10:8–9. Using information from this passage and from Numbers 8:5–22, make a list of the Levites' duties.

Language Notes

Malachi 2:5

English: **fear/reverence/awe**
Hebrew: *mora'* (from the root *yare'*)
Definition: fear, reverence, terror

English: **fear/reverence/awe**
Hebrew: *yare'*
Definition: to fear, be afraid; to stand in awe of, be awed; to fear, reverence, honor, respect

English: **fear/reverence/awe**
Hebrew: *chathath*
Definition: to be shattered, be dismayed, be broken, be abolished, be afraid

Now read Malachi 2:1–9. Remember, today we want to highlight the Levites' good beginning, so focus, for now, on verses 5–7. What was God's purpose in establishing a covenant with the Levites?

What would this covenant require from the Levites?

What would be the positive results in the lives of the people if the Levites kept the covenant (vv. 6–7)?

The Levites had a vital role in the success of Israel as God's chosen people. Look back at Malachi 2:5. This verse contains three different Hebrew words that describe the attitude that the priest/Levite in covenant with God had to have. Depending on your translation, they may appear as forms of *fear, reverence,* or *awe.*

Review the meanings of the three descriptive words from Malachi 2:5. They are listed in the language notes (previous page) in the order in which they appear in the verse.

It is obvious the attitude described in verse 5 is the attitude that God commends. In fact, the covenantal promises of this verse—life and peace—were dependent on the Levites' obedience stemming from an attitude of godly fear. Those Levites who were originally in covenant with God feared Him and, therefore, obeyed Him. God was pleased with them.

There is a phrase in verse 6 that I don't want us to miss because it reminds me of some other men of faith who pleased God. Malachi tells us that these obedient Levites *"walked with"* God. *Walked* is translated from the Hebrew verb *halak.* (See language notes for Malachi 2:6 on the next page.) However, according to the *Theological Wordbook of the Old Testament,* the word is used frequently in the Old Testament to describe also the people's idolatry. They were "going after" other or false gods. In contrast, the righteous were said to be "going after" God. [1]

The Bible uses this same Hebrew word, *halak*, to describe other champions of faith in the Old Testament, notably Enoch and Noah.

The Bible describes Enoch, one of the members of the Hebrews "Hall of Faith," as one who *"walked with God"* (Genesis 5:24). We are told in Hebrews 11:5 that Enoch was *"commended as one who pleased God."* In fact, he pleased God so much that God took him from this life without Enoch experiencing death. Imagine that!

Read Genesis 6:8–9 to find out about another member of the Hall of Faith who walked with God. See language notes for Genesis 6:9 for information on the three Hebrew words used to describe Noah in verse 9. They are listed in the order they appear in the Scripture.
Compare Genesis 6:9 with Hebrews 11:7. List the words and phrases that describe Noah's character and the kind of relationship he had with God.

One word that the New International Version uses to describe Noah is *blameless*. The Hebrew word translated as "blameless" in Genesis 6:9 is *tamiym* and can also be translated as "without blemish." This same term describes God's expectations for the condition of sacrifices, as we studied last week. They had to be *tamiym*, without blemish.

Noah was *tamiym*. His life was the kind of sacrifice God desires. Noah found favor in the eyes of the God with whom he walked. The original covenant Levites, described in Malachi 2:5–6, also walked with God. They would never have offered God blemished sacrifices, because they feared Him. Unfortunately, as we will see tomorrow, their descendants had lost their fear of God.

Language Notes

Malachi 2:6

English: **walk/walked with**
Hebrew: *halak* (found also in Genesis 6:9)
Definition: to go, walk, come, depart, proceed, move, go away

Genesis 6:9

English: **righteous**
Hebrew: *tsaddiyq*
Definition: just, lawful, righteous

English: **blameless/without blemish**
Hebrew: *tamiym*
Definition: complete, whole, entire, sound

English: **walk/walked with**
Hebrew: *halak* (as discussed in reference to Malachi 2:6)
Definition: to go, walk, come, depart, proceed, move, go away

Today, we have looked at lives that pleased God: the original covenant Levites, Enoch, and Noah. In some way, they were all leaders. Although not without sin, they lived lives without blemish and obediently fulfilled God's purposes for them because they feared God. What about us?

> List the leadership roles God has entrusted to you. Include also the responsibilities you have outside the walls of the church. For example, you may be a parent or have an influential role in your community. What is your attitude toward God as you serve in these roles? How can you demonstrate a fear for God through these roles?

DAY 2

Lack of Fear in New Generation

One of the things I enjoyed about living in Alberta near the Canadian Rockies was the easy access to ski areas. We could be at our favorite resort in less than an hour. I am a decent skier. In fact, I love to ski. It's the falling down I hate. I am usually cautious, so I don't fall down very often. But when I do, it is spectacular. Most often I fall right under the chair lift. Why? Pride. As I said, I am usually cautious. But when I am skiing under the lift, I start to think about the fact that people may be watching. I want to look good, of course, so I allow myself to pick up speed. I make quicker, shorter turns instead of wider, slower (safer) turns. And just when I think I must really look impressive to the folks floating overhead, it's over…and over and over and over. The results are bruised body parts and a busted ego.

The Bible is very clear on the issue of how God feels about pride. We are going to take a closer look at this issue later in the study, but I bring it up here because I believe pride was at least partially to blame for the Levites' failure in leadership. In Henry and Richard Blackaby's book *Spiritual Leadership*, the authors cite pride as one of a leader's worst enemies. "Pride causes Christian leaders to take the credit not only for what their people have done but also for what God has accomplished. Spiritual leaders are God's servants, but pride can cause them to act as if God were their servant, obligated to answer their selfish prayers and to bless their grandiose schemes."[2] This certainly seems to be the case in Malachi.

In Malachi 2, God compared the original, "fearful," obedient Levites to the blemished Levites practicing in the days of Malachi. Let's do the same.

Read Malachi 2:1–9. As you read this passage, fill out table 5. Include all behaviors, attitudes, and character traits that are explicit or implied.

Table 5. Comparison between original Levites and those written about in Malachi

	ORIGINAL LEVITES	LEVITES IN MALACHI'S DAY
Attitudes		
Actions		
Results		

What evidence do you see that pride may have been a cause for the Levites' failure?

What other possible reasons for their disobedience and failure do you see in this passage?

As we discussed yesterday, God's original purpose in establishing a covenant with the Levites was to bring life and peace. God desired to bless not only the Levites but also the entire nation of Israel through their obedience. The original covenant Levites, who were obedient to God's commands, became a channel of blessing for a whole nation. The Levites of Malachi's day were not obedient; they did not keep the covenant with God.

Based on Malachi 2:1–9 and the insight you gained from the table you just completed, what do you think the Israelites of Malachi's day were experiencing instead of life and peace?

Yesterday when we read Deuteronomy 10:8, we learned that the pronouncement of blessing was a duty for the Levites. This is significant to understanding this portion of Malachi. This priestly blessing is found in Numbers.

Read Numbers 6:22–27. Based on verse 27, what was the purpose of the priestly blessing? And, significantly, who has the authority and power to actually bestow the blessing?

Please read again Malachi 2:1–4. What command of God had the Levites/priests obviously not kept? If they did not immediately repent, what would be the consequences of their sin?

The Hebrew word translated as "blessings" in Malachi 2:2 is *berakah*. It is from the root word *barak*, which we find in Numbers 6:22–27. According to the *Theological Wordbook of the Old Testament, to bless* means "to endue with power for success, prosperity, fecundity, longevity, etc." The Bible recognizes God as the only source of blessing. It is in His name only that the Levites/priests were able to confer blessing on others. "As a result, those who are wrongly related to God can neither bless nor be blessed."[3]

The Levites/priests addressed in Malachi 2 had failed to give honor to God and His name before the people. And just whom do you suppose they sought to honor instead? (Here is where I see pride rearing its ugly head.) Therefore, their role as spiritual leaders was not only ineffective but cursed by God (v. 2). Because the priests had dishonored God, He would dishonor them before the people (v. 3).

The terms *dung, offal,* or *refuse* (depending on your translation) refer to the material inside the intestines of animals that were sacrificed as a sin offering during religious festivals. This material was to be carried outside of the camp with the hide, meat, head, legs, and internal organs to be burned (Leviticus 4:12). Because the animal had been used as a sin offering—meaning the sin of the individual had been symbolically transferred to the animal—it was unclean. God used this imagery to describe how He would bring dishonor to the priests/Levites. Because of their sin, God saw these Levites as unclean and unacceptable. They deserved to be treated as dung and carried off outside the camp. Wow! God takes sin, especially in His leaders, extremely seriously.

We also learn from Malachi 2:5–9 that although the original covenant Levites feared God and His name, the current generation of Levites/priests did not. As you read the passage, it is obvious that godly fear was the key to the successful fulfillment of the original Levites' covenant role.

From what you have learned in this study so far, do you believe that Christians today should fear God? Why or why not?

I hope you are beginning to get a clearer picture of the biblical meaning of godly fear. Although I still have questions about what this should look like played out in the life of a believer, I am convinced that *yare'* describes the proper response of any individual to his or her holy Creator. I am convinced because it is what I see in God's Word:

> *"You must fear the LORD your God and serve him."*
> —Deuteronomy 6:13 (NLT)

If we truly have an attitude of godly fear, it will be reflected in the way we live our lives before God. We will continue to explore this truth together throughout the rest of this study.

Before close of today's Bible study session, take a moment to ask God to mold your heart and mind into conformity with His will. Record any insights He gives you.

DAY 3

God's New Covenant Priests

According to the Association of American Publishers, the sales of religious books grew 14.2 percent compounded annually from 2002 to 2005.[4] While this category includes many topics other than Christianity, the statistics reveal that Americans are increasingly seeking information about spiritual matters. The wide availability of this type of material is wonderful. There is a great need for sound Bible teachers to help and encourage us on our road to spiritual maturity. However, I wonder if this also reveals a tendency I experienced in my own life.

Years ago, God showed me something that changed my relationship with Him. The Bible studies I was doing had become the focus of my time with Him. My Christian growth was based primarily on what God had taught someone else. Rarely did I just pick up God's Word, without human direction, and allow the Holy Spirit to teach me. Now my time with God begins with just the two of us. I read His Word and allow Him to teach me directly. Then I supplement my spiritual education with the wonderful truths that God has to show me through His gifted teachers.

Do you look first and foremost to Christ and His leadership, or do you rely too heavily on someone else? You are a member of God's holy priesthood (1 Peter 2:9). Every believer has the Spirit of Christ. He is our Counselor and Teacher (John 14:26). Because of this wonderful truth, believers are able to learn directly from God (John 16:13–15)!

Let's always remember the position we have before God through Christ. The Levites of the Old Covenant were charged with the task of passing the truth they received from God on to the people (Malachi 2:6). Yet under the New Covenant, believers have direct access to the Father. As believers, we are priests before God. Our role comes with responsibilities as well as privileges. That is our focus of today's study.

Please read 1 Peter 2:4–5, 9–10. Scan the passage again and make a list of all the words and phrases that describe your position as a believer in Christ.

What similarities do you see between this passage in 1 Peter and what you've learned from Malachi?

Remember that the Levites were in covenant with God. The Hebrew word translated as "covenant" is *beriyth*. It is derived from a root word, *karath*, which means "to cut." In fact, in the Old Testament, *beriyth* (covenant) is usually used in conjunction with *karath* (to cut) when referring to the act of two parties entering into a contract or agreement. The making or "cutting" of covenants involved the ritual of a bloody animal sacrifice.

Malachi 2:5 tells us that God's purpose for His covenant with the Levites was to bring the people life and peace. These original covenant Levites obeyed God's Word and guarded His covenant (Deuteronomy 33:9). They were faithful to uphold and guide the people in the covenant God cut with the nation of Israel. Like the Levites and the nation of Israel, believers have entered into a covenant with God. We are, in fact, priests of the New Covenant. Let's take a look.

Read Hebrews 9:16–28. How was the Old Covenant put into effect?

What were its limitations?

How was the New Covenant put into effect?

How is the New Covenant superior to the Old Covenant?

Jesus Christ is the Mediator of the New Covenant between God and mankind. His intercessory death put the covenant into effect. Jesus was the sacrifice used to cut the new and lasting covenant. Our holy God provided for us what He demanded from us—the death penalty for our sin. God's love working together with His justice provided a way for us to be reconciled to Him. If we have responded to Christ's sacrificial death and been reconciled to God, we are His priests under His New Covenant. Now how should we respond?

Read 2 Corinthians 5:18–21. What responsibilities do we have as priests of the New Covenant?

Malachi 2:5 states that God's purpose for the covenant with the Levites was to bring life and peace. Review 2 Corinthians 5:18–21 with this in mind. In this latter passage, what evidence do you see that God's purposes have not changed?

🕊 **As we end today, reflect on the faithfulness of the original covenant Levites. God commended them for their godly fear, their obedience, and the way they guarded His covenant. As a priest of God's New Covenant, in what ways can your life demonstrate the same faithfulness?**

DAY 4

The New Covenant Call

In 1991, I was on a missions trip with a women's group to the recently dissolved Soviet Union. One evening, we checked into a hotel in Bishkek, a city in the former Soviet republic of Kirghizia (Kyrgyzstan). It was already dark when we arrived. Based on the noise, the volume of people, and the coming and going, the hotel bar was a popular spot with guests and locals.

As my roommate and I began to settle in for the night, we noticed our room was a bit isolated. By chance, it was separated from the block of rooms down the hall where the rest of our group stayed. Also, there was no phone in the room.

We both went to sleep fairly quickly but were awakened sometime in the night by the loud voices of two men in the room next to ours. They had obviously been patrons of the hotel bar that evening. As we listened, they moved from their room out into the hall and began to pound on our door. The shouting intensified, and we clearly understood one word in the midst of the Russian: "Americans." Even though neither of us spoke a word of Russian, it didn't take a translator to know their intentions were not friendly.

For the next hour or more, the men alternated between shouting at us through the wall between our rooms and attempting in various ways to get through our door. They even tried jimmying the lock and throwing their bodies against it to break it down. Miraculously, the fragile-looking door held firm.

Afraid to even leave our beds, my roommate and I whispered to each other and prayed fervently. After a while, the Holy Spirit prompted me to pray in a very specific way: "Lord, use the alcohol, which these men have so obviously consumed in vast quantities, to either put them to sleep or cause them to pass out." Within three minutes, it went from angry shouting to complete silence! The Lord was our Protector.

This horrible experience affected the way I behaved for the next few days. I was very nervous around the local men and wouldn't make eye contact with any of them. I believed that they all hated Americans and would do whatever was necessary to run us off. Of course, this was all a faulty exaggeration brought on by a fearful experience, but it shows that fear can shape our attitudes and behavior.

Recall our discussion about phobias from week 1, day 1. Abnormal or misplaced fear can negatively impact and impede our lives. Over and over again in the Scriptures, God assures us that we need not fear other people, the circumstances of life, or even death. He is our Provider and Protector. *"Even when I walk through the dark valley of death, I will not be afraid, for you are close beside me. Your rod and your staff protect and comfort me"* (Psalm 23:4 NLT).

Read Psalm 34:4–10. (***Note:*** The word *yare'* is found once in verse 7 and twice in verse 9.)

David wrote this psalm to express his thankfulness and praise to God for his deliverance in a particular situation. But it is not a blanket promise that God will cause everything in our lives to turn out the way we want.

Look back at Psalm 34:4–10. What promises do you find in this passage?

Are conditions stated? If so, what are they?

A passage in the New Testament—Matthew 10—provides us with further insight. Jesus commissioned the twelve apostles to go out as His ambassadors to spread the news about the kingdom of God. Before He sent them out, He prepared them for the circumstances they would face. Some of the people they would be going to would receive the news of the kingdom gladly, and others would reject it. In fact, some would persecute them because of the message they brought.

Read Matthew 10:17–33. What dangerous circumstances would the apostles encounter? Would they be physically rescued from all of these?

Review verses 17 and 26, then compare them with Matthew 10:16. What attitude were the apostles to have toward their persecutors, and how were they to prepare for almost certain danger?

What does it mean to be *"as shrewd as snakes and as innocent as doves"* (Matthew 10:16)? As Christians, we should not invite or foolishly provoke persecution; however, we must not allow the fear of it to prevent us from complete obedience to God's will. There is a balance. We must be straightforward and sincere, yet wise and watchful. When God called me to go on the missions trip to the former Soviet Union, I trusted in His protection and obeyed even though the country was in the midst of turmoil. Yet I did not wander off alone, and I locked the door at night!

Please reread Matthew 10:28–33. The word translated as "afraid" or "fear" is the Greek verb *phobeo*. Does that sound familiar? It means "to put to flight; to terrify, frighten." According to Matthew 10:28–33, why should we not fear what men can do to us? Look through the entire passage for reasons.

If we are not to fear what people might do to us, why should we fear what God can do?

God is aware of every aspect of our lives. He knows when my son falls and scrapes his knee, and He knows when my heart is broken from grief. He knows when my neighbor rejects my invitation to church and when my husband is passed by for a promotion at work because he lives his faith.

What this passage from Matthew 10 teaches us is that fear of people or potentially negative circumstances must not keep us from completely obeying God. In fact, just the opposite is true. Our fear of God must motivate us to obey God rather than man. Godly fear is fostered when we, as individuals, not only recognize the holiness of God and His eternal purposes over the temporal nature of the things of earth, but also allow this recognition to affect how we live our lives. Yes, it is Christ's love that compels us to spread the good news of the kingdom of God, but it is godly fear that keeps us moving forward when the fear of man would stop us in our tracks.

I believe it was this unbeatable combination of love and fear that strengthened Rachel Joy Scott on April 20, 1999, when two of her fellow students at Columbine High School in Littleton, Colorado, opened fire. Richard Castaldo, a friend of Rachel's, was shot that day but survived and told Rachel's story soon after the tragedy.

> According to Richard's earliest account, he and Rachel were sitting outside when they saw [Eric] Harris and [Dylan] Klebold approaching. Without warning, the two young men opened fire, severing Richard's spine and shooting Rachel twice in her legs and once in her torso.
>
> As Richard lay stunned and Rachel attempted to crawl to safety, the shooters began to walk away, only to return seconds later. At that point, Harris reportedly grabbed Rachel by her hair, held her head up, and asked her the question: "Do you believe in God?"
>
> "You know I do," replied Rachel.
>
> "Then go be with Him," responded Harris before shooting her in the head.[5]
>
> —Darrell Scott and Beth Nimmo, with Steve Rabey, *Rachel's Tears*

God used Rachel Scott's courageous testimony for His own glory. Whether God protects us *from* or carries us *through* persecution and difficulties, it is

His divine prerogative to orchestrate our lives' circumstances to serve His eternal purposes.

> 🕊 **Will you fearfully trust God in and through every circumstance of your life? Will you live your life in constant acknowledgment of your Lord and in complete obedience, no matter the circumstances? Write a prayer to God that expresses your commitment, doubts, and fears.**

DAY 5

A Covenant of the Heart

We've all heard the old saying, "Just going through the motions." I remember one frustrating moment of parenting that now serves as a funny example. Sarah, my middle child, was 7 or 8. We had made plans for the family to go out together, and Sarah did not want to go. When we informed her that she had no choice and was indeed going, she replied, "Well, you can make me go, but you can't make me like it." And she was right.

There was a time in my life when, spiritually, I was just going through the motions. When I was a child, my Christian parents took me to church and taught me about God. When I was 8, I understood that I was a sinner and that Jesus willingly gave His life to pay the debt I owed. For the next 18 years, I went through the spiritual motions. I went to church regularly. I was active in the youth group and the choir. As a young adult, I taught children's Sunday School. From all outward appearances, I was a devoted follower of Christ.

But I knew I was missing something. My heart was not right before God. Kathy was still in control. The turning point came when I was 26. Through a women's Bible study on the Book of Romans, God showed me that in order to experience new life in Christ, I had to die to self and give Him control. I had been trying to be a Christian from the outside in. Now God could begin to make me like Christ from the inside out.

Our churches today are filled with people who are outwardly participating in the trappings of religion, but have not experienced death to self followed by new life in Christ. Putting on a religious front is not just a current-day happening. The Levites in the Book of Malachi were doing it. Their hearts were not right before God. And more than 400 years later, Jesus confronted the Pharisees over the same issue.

Jesus throughout His ministry warned the crowd that, as a whole, the Pharisees were not the righteous leaders they made themselves out to be (Matthew 23:1–3, for example). And Jesus confronted some of these leaders with their hypocrisy. He presented seven woes, or warnings, to the Pharisees concerning their behavior, as recorded in Matthew 23, beginning with verse 13. This "woe formula" is reminiscent of the blessings and curses God set before the nation of Israel, as recorded in Deuteronomy 27–28. If the people were obedient, keeping God's covenant, then He would bless them (Deuteronomy 28:1–2). However, if they were disobedient to the covenant, they would experience curses (Deuteronomy 28:15).

Please read Matthew 23:23–28. What evidence do you see in this passage that the Pharisees took God's law seriously?

What evidence do you see that suggests they were legalistically going through the motions, but their hearts were not right before God? (*Note:* The gnat and the camel were both considered unclean animals for Israel and, therefore, were not to be consumed.)

Jesus called the Pharisees *"blind guides"* in verse 24. Compare this to Malachi 2:8. Describe the possible impact of this kind of leadership.

The Old Covenant, the one God cut with Israel on Mount Sinai, was glorious. God came to dwell with men. He established a way by which His people could be in relationship with Him. But this covenant was merely a shadow of the superior covenant that was to come. Every element of the Old Covenant—the tabernacle, the sacrifices, the priesthood, the Law—was representative of the New Covenant in Christ (Hebrews 9:23–26). The Old Covenant and its law were designed by God to make us recognize our need for a Savior and to point us to Christ (Galatians 3:22–25). Christ did not come to abolish the Law, but instead to fulfill it completely (Matthew 5:17). The first covenant was external. The second would be internal.

Read Hebrews 8:6–12. Why is the New Covenant superior to the Old Covenant?

Look again at verse 10. What difference does it make that under the New Covenant, God's law is written on the heart instead of tablets of stone?

Read Matthew 5:17–20 and scan verses 21–40 for further context. If, as Christians, we are no longer under the Law, explain Jesus's expectations found in this passage.

The external practice of religion is merely a human undertaking powered by self. It is not true Christianity. We can keep up appearances for only so long. The Old Covenant focused primarily on the external, but the New Covenant mediated by Christ goes deeper and deals with the heart. When we enter into the New Covenant with Christ by exchanging our lives of sin for His life of righteousness, we receive the Holy Spirit. It is the Spirit who then transforms our hearts and minds, empowering us to be obedient to God (Romans 8:9–14).

What about you? Do you ever feel as if you are simply going through the motions of a religion and not living a faith? Ask God to examine your heart and reveal any areas in which you still maintain control. If God has shown you something specific today, describe it below. Will you pray now and surrender this area of your life to Him?

WEEK 5

GOD DENOUNCES
WORLDLY COMPROMISE

I have two teenage daughters. That makes me a referee. I have had to settle disputes between them since before the youngest was old enough to crawl. However, the older they got, the more I refused to intervene and began to encourage them to work out their problems themselves. I began to teach them the fine art of compromise. Give and take. *The American Heritage Dictionary of the English Language* lists the first definition for the noun use of *compromise* as "a settlement of differences in which each side makes concessions."[1]

We are often told that compromise is a vital element in any successful relationship, including relationships with siblings, friends, co-workers, and spouses. But what role, if any, should compromise play in the relationship between God and mankind, between the Creator and the created? I have often tried it: "Lord, I know that gossip is wrong, but this isn't really gossip. I need to let Susan know what is going on so she can pray for this situation." Yet when it comes to the relationship between the Master and one of His children, *compromise* by the child is just a dressed-up word for "disobedience."

The American Heritage Dictionary lists another definition for the verb form of *compromise:* "to expose or make liable to danger, suspicion, or disrepute."[2] This week in our study of Malachi, we will see how compromise in the lives of God's people threatened to bring disaster. Let's pray we learn this lesson from example rather than from personal experience!

DAY 1

Uncompromised Obedience Required

My husband and I have established rules, curfews, and chores galore for our three children. For example, those two teenage daughters I told you about are not allowed to have any male friends in the house unless a parent is home. They think we are overcautious. We know the rule is for their protection.

God also gives commands and establishes boundaries for our protection. Like my daughters, we may think that sometimes God is overcautious or maybe even out of step with the times. We may be tempted to compromise God's timeless commands in favor of a more society-friendly or contemporary stance. But the all-knowing God knows what is best for His children.

Please read Malachi 2:10–16. In the passage previous to this one, God was speaking to the priests/Levites. To whom was the prophet speaking in this passage?

What areas of compromise are identified? (**Note:** Although Malachi specifically deals with the topic of divorce, we will focus on the more general problem of sin through compromise.)

Reread Malachi 2:7–8, which we studied last week. Do you think this passage has any bearing on the situation in verses 10–16? If so, how?

Obviously, God holds His leaders accountable for the results of sinful leadership. However, even under poor leadership, every individual is also responsible to God for his or her own behavior. In Malachi 2:10, the prophet reminded the people that they were a covenant family under God the Father. Their disobedience not only affected their covenant relationship with God, but it also destroyed the covenant of unity and faith they had with one another.

Most Bible scholars agree that Malachi 2:10–16 refers to a literal situation. The Israelite men were divorcing the Israelite wives of their youth and remarrying women from the surrounding nations who worshipped false gods. We will look at the historical background that supports and demonstrates this literal interpretation. There are a few scholars, however, who believe the passage is a spiritual situation. They assert that the Israelites of Malachi's day had turned away from Jehovah, their first love, and gone after pagan gods. Based on the historical context of Malachi, I believe that the situation was both literal and spiritual.

Either way, the results were the same. The Israelites had compromised in their obedience to God. Historically, this particular compromise led to idolatry—just as God had warned them from the beginning. Nearly 1,000 years before Malachi, when the Israelites were positioned to enter the Promised Land, Moses reminded them of God's commands and the conditions of God's covenant with them.

Read Deuteronomy 7:1–6. What divine commands to the Israelites are found in this passage?

What was the purpose of these commands?

In what ways were these commands for the good of the Israelites?

God first gave these commands to the Israelites when they were camped at the foot of Mount Sinai, not long after they left Egypt (Exodus 34:11–16). If the occasion in Malachi was the first time the Israelites had ignored God in this matter, I might be tempted to say, "Well, they obeyed for a thousand years before they slipped up. That's better than I could do." But this wasn't the first time. In fact, the Book of Numbers records an incident that occurred a mere 40 years after God gave this command.

Read Numbers 25:1–3, and take note of the downward cycle of sin. Describe how the initial sin led to outright idolatry.

Read Numbers 25:4–9. How did God respond to the disobedience of these people?

Let's jump forward in Israel's history to the reign of King Solomon.

Read 1 Kings 11:1–8. In this passage, what was Solomon's first act of compromise with the commands of God?

Describe how this act of disobedience led him further away from God.

Unfortunately, the Israelites in the days of Malachi did not learn completely from their ancestors' mistakes. Compromise with God's command concerning intermarriage with the pagan nations led to blatant idolatry. God disciplined His children time and again to turn their hearts back to Him. But their disobedience was persistent. In response, God brought the destruction of both the nations of Israel and Judah. But in His faithfulness, He preserved a holy remnant and brought them back to Jerusalem from exile. The books of Ezra and Nehemiah record the history of this remnant. (Malachi was a prophet during the same time in history.) Did the remnant learn from the mistakes of their ancestors?

Read Ezra 9:1–2. Once again, describe the sin of the people. List all who were participating in this disobedience.

Our family loves to camp. We have been camping together since our children were very young. One Memorial Day weekend many years ago, we went camping in southeast New Mexico with friends. Our son, Mark, not quite three at the time, was the youngest of the group. We set up camp at the bottom of a heavily wooded slope. That hillside quickly became a magnet for all six children. The oldest four began to build a fort, while the two "babies" pestered them. The four parents decided that for the kids' protection, some rules regarding the hill needed to be established. The most important rule, due to the steep grade, was this: no running on the way down.

Because Mark was so young, we watched him closely and tried to remind him to walk every time he started down the hill. On one fateful descent, he chose not to completely follow the rules. He wasn't really running, but he sure wasn't walking either. All it took was one small branch in his path to send him sliding down headfirst, on his face, about halfway to the bottom. When we reached the screaming boy, we discovered his face and forearms were covered in scratches and scrapes. A small compromise of the rule started a big downhill slide.

Compromise with the world is a slippery slope. Sometimes even one small step off God's perfect path can be the beginning of a disastrous tumble. No one is immune. As we have already seen today in Numbers and 1 Kings, all of God's people—from the common Israelites to the leaders to the king—were guilty. How could they have avoided their fall into idolatry? By obeying God's command not to marry pagan women. It seems like a no-brainer. Yet even with the ready availability of God's Word to guide and warn, many Christians today fall into the trap of compromise.

List some contemporary examples of how seemingly minor compromises could lead Christians to fall deep into disobedience.

Did you notice how God's expectations for His people did not change over the centuries? God declares, *"I am the LORD, and I do not change"* (Malachi 3:6 NLT). Yet how many of God's commands would we like to see updated with the times?

As we end today, ask God to reveal to you any of His commands you have disregarded as outdated. Record below anything He shows you.

DAY 2

Disastrous Consequences of Worldly Compromise

All behavior, good or bad, brings consequences. According to the Bible, we reap what we sow:

> *Do not be deceived: God cannot be mocked. A man reaps what he sows. The one who sows to please his sinful nature, from that nature will reap destruction; the one who sows to please the Spirit, from the Spirit will reap eternal life.*
>
> —Galatians 6:7–8

This truth applies to nature (I have never seen petunias come up from marigold seeds) and humanity. For instance, disobedience to God's commands is seed for bringing forth disastrous consequences.

Reread Malachi 2:10–16. Make a list below of all the negative behaviors or disobedient actions of which God accused His people.

Now let's consider the consequences of those actions. Make a list of every consequence you can find in this passage, whether you would consider it natural or handed down by God.

We will spend the rest of today highlighting a couple of these consequences. Even under the New Covenant of grace, our disobedience still brings consequences. I believe that, as Christians, we take sin more seriously when we consider its potential and very real repercussions.

In chapter 2, the first consequence Malachi pronounced was that those who had been unfaithful to God and the community should be cut off (v. 12). We examined this Hebrew word for "cut off," *karath*, in week 4, day 3. God had "cut a covenant" with the nation of Israel. In their disobedience, individuals had broken this covenant by marrying foreign women and allowing them to lead them to worship other gods (v. 11). The phrase in verse 12, *"even though he brings offerings to the LORD Almighty,"* reveals that the sinners were unrepentant; they were worshipping Jehovah and false gods simultaneously.

In Malachi 2:12, God issued a warning to these unrepentant covenant breakers. If they didn't return to obedience, God would excommunicate them from His community, cutting them off from His covenant and its benefits.

In Malachi 2:10–16, we are warned about another consequence of worldly compromise. Verses 13–16 describe persons who were living in unrepentant sin, yet were upset because God neither paid attention to nor accepted their offerings.

Read Isaiah 59:1–2. How does this passage help explain what was happening in Malachi 2:10–16?

Divine silence does not always mean an individual has allowed unrestrained sin to interfere with his or her relationship with God. But sometimes it does. God's answer to this predicament is repentance and complete obedience. First John 1:9 states, *"If we confess our sins, he is faithful and just and will forgive us our sins and purify us from all unrighteousness."* If I am experiencing a time of silence from God, the first thing I do is ask Him to search my heart and mind and reveal any sin in my life. If sin is the reason for God's silence, nothing else will happen until it is dealt a deathblow.

The New Testament also has a lot to say about compromise with the world. In fact, a passage in the Book of James has several parallels with today's passage in Malachi.

Read James 4:1–5. List the similarities between James's audience and Malachi's audience.

What phrase in verse 4 reveals that James's readers had also compromised in their obedience to God?

According to this passage, what is the consequence for someone who becomes a friend of the world?

Worldly compromise is serious business. Because God is righteously jealous of those who belong to Him, He often allows us to suffer the consequences of our disobedience. His purpose, however, is not our pain or discomfort, but rather our repentance and return to Him.

Read James 4:6–10. Describe how persons who have disobediently compromised with the world can restore their intimate fellowship with God.

God desires to have a continually close relationship with each of us—one that is unhindered by the sin of worldly compromise. Unfortunately, all of us sometimes choose our own way over God's. Yet in His grace, God uses even the consequences of our sin to draw us back to Him. Are you currently experiencing intimacy with your heavenly Father, or have the consequences of worldly compromise strained your relationship with Him? In tomorrow's lesson, we are going to ask God to examine our lives.

Before you close your book today, will you ask God to prepare your heart to hear what He has to say tomorrow?

Day 3

Areas of Compromise

Many years ago, when my oldest daughter had just turned one, I quit my full-time paying job to be a full-time mom. I loved being home with Kelley and would make the same decision again. Kelley was a great sleeper. When she was eight weeks old, she began sleeping through the night. As a one-year-old, she was also taking a four-hour nap every afternoon. The only problem with that was I didn't know what to do with myself.

We lived in a small house that took me about 23 minutes to clean. I had just quit my job, so I had not yet gotten involved in any organizations or ministries that needed my attention. So unfortunately, I began to watch the daytime soap operas. I am not saying soap operas are inherently evil, but I became addicted to the ongoing story line. The devil had found an area of weakness in me.

Before long, I was arranging my entire daily schedule around two particular shows. If Kelley didn't fall asleep on schedule, I became frustrated and angry. Not only that, but my guilty secret led me to other sin. I knew Marsha, my Christian friend and neighbor, would not approve of my soap opera habit. If she called just before or during one of my shows, I would make up an excuse to get off the phone. Wait. Let me be honest. The excuses I offered weren't excuses; they were blatant lies to cover up activity of which I was ashamed.

Right now you may be thinking that watching soap operas really isn't all that bad. I would have to say it depends on the brand of soap. Christians should consider how the content of everything we watch on television measures up to God's standards. But that wasn't the only issue here.

Jesus told the Jewish religious leaders that all of God's commandments hang on just two: *"'Love the Lord your God with all your heart and with all your soul and with all your mind.' This is the first and greatest commandment. And the second is like it: 'Love your neighbor as yourself'"* (Matthew 22:37–39). These words of Jesus's provide a great tool we can use to evaluate any behavior, attitude, or thought. My soap opera activity did not measure up very well. Not only did I lie to my neighbor and lose patience with my baby, but in the process, I also transgressed against a holy God.

After going on like this for a while, God clearly impressed a message on my heart: "Stop watching those shows, and stop it now!" I have not always obeyed God immediately and completely, but this time I did. I said, "Yes, Lord," and quit cold turkey. Unfortunately, every sin area in my life has not been so easy to set aside.

In the course of writing this study, God has shown me several areas in which I am still gratifying the desires of my sinful nature and compromising with the world. Attitudes such as pride and selfishness still have a foothold in my life. They affect my relationship with God and other people. This kind of deep-seated sin is not as easy to turn off as the television. But, praise God, He offers forgiveness and healing when we turn to Him in repentance and submission. And *"He who began a good work in [me] will carry it on to completion"* (Philippians 1:6).

Do you earnestly desire for God to make you more like Christ? If so, you must grant Him full access to every area of your life. Today, and at other times in this study, we are going to ask God to examine our lives and begin to show us any areas of compromise. Our lives should be open books before God and His scrutiny.

Before we start, let me encourage you. God continues to work on His children throughout their entire lives. We will never be completely what God desires us to be until we see Him face-to-face (1 John 3:2). However, we must continually *"press on"* toward God's goal for us (Philippians 3:14). Whether today marks the beginning in that direction or another step along the road, *press on!*

Right now spend a few moments in prayer. Ask God to open your ears and prepare your heart for whatever He wants to show you today. Ask Him to examine your life. Ask Him to use His Word as a catalyst to reveal areas of sin in your life.

Now turn to Psalm 139:23–24, and read it. If that passage expresses your desire, state it out loud as your prayer to God.

Make a list of the ways in which you spend your time. Include jobs, hobbies, social activities, sports, community involvement, church activities, relationships, and anything else that fills your life.

The night Jesus was betrayed, He prayed for His followers. *"My prayer is not that you take them out of the world but that you protect them from the evil one. They are not of the world, even as I am not of it. Sanctify them by the truth; your word is truth. As you sent me into the world, I have sent them into the world"* (John 17:15–18). Although God does not want us to be *like* the world and its ways, He does want us to be *in* the world, revealing Christ to the lost. Our goal, then, is to allow God to purge our lives of worldly influence so we can influence the world.

Read Ephesians 4:17 through 5:7. While there is no exhaustive list of sin in Scripture, this passage can help us identify some worldly influence. Use what you find in this Ephesians passage to fill in table 6.

Table 6. Worldly influence

WORLDLY ATTITUDES	WORLDLY BEHAVIORS

Now in light of the table you just filled in, examine the list of activities you made earlier in today's session. Have any of these worldly attitudes or behaviors crept into any area of your life? Evaluate all this in light of what Jesus stated to be the two greatest commandments: to love God and to love other people. How does each identified attitude, behavior, or activity affect your relationship with God? With other people?

As we close today, reflect on Psalm 86:11. Will you join me as I ask God to give me a heart that is completely uncompromised before Him? Write your prayer below.

DAY 4

Corporate Compromise

Jumbo shrimp, old news, working vacation, deafening silence, and rolling stop—these phrases, known as oxymora, are examples of seemingly contradictory terms that really do have meaning for those of us who use them. But how do the terms *private faith* and *independent Christian* strike you? Have you ever heard, or perhaps even used, these or similar expressions? In *Experiencing God Together*, Henry and Melvin Blackaby state that a believer's "relationship with God is personal, but it was never meant to be private."[3]

While it is true that God saves us individually and relates to each of His children personally, He never meant for us to live the Christian life independently. Every new believer is born into the spiritual family of Christ. God has designated and designed the local church to be the place where believers are to be nurtured and taught and encouraged to serve and to grow to spiritual maturity. The Blackabys elaborate: "We cannot live our faith in isolation; that would run contrary to the purpose of God's salvation."[4]

Read Malachi 2:10. How does this verse emphasize the family relationship between believers?

As members of God's family, we are connected not only to God but also to one another. The sinful way in which the people described in Malachi were treating each other revealed something about the nature of their relationship to the Father. In *Thru the Bible with J. Vernon McGee*, McGee comments on Malachi 2:10: "Now here they were, a chosen people, yet breaking God's covenant and dealing treacherously one with the other. They were not right with God, and so they were not right with each other."[5] This unique relationship also means that even one or two members of a body can either positively or negatively affect the entire body (1 Corinthians 12:26). Let's look at an earlier incident during Israel's history that serves as another excellent example of this truth.

Read Joshua 6:17–19. What specific command did God give the Israelites regarding the plunder of Jericho?

Scan all of Joshua 7, paying particular attention to verses 1, 11–12, and 24–26. How many people disobeyed God's command regarding the plunder of Jericho, and how many were held accountable by God?

What were the consequences?

How was Israel's relationship with Jehovah restored?

Achan did not fear God enough to take His command seriously. His desire for material things was stronger than his desire to be obedient. An entire nation suffered negative consequences because of the compromise of one man. This account demonstrates vital truths about the nature of the body of Christ. First, each member of the body is accountable *to* and *for* every other member. Second, sin in the body, even hidden sin, affects the body's ability to be effective for the kingdom of God.

> In your personal reflection time during yesterday's study, did you identify anything in your own life that could be negatively affecting the body of Christ?

How should the church respond if one or more of its members are involved in blatant or unconfessed sin? Let's revisit a passage in Ezra we read on day 1 of this week. The Book of Ezra covers roughly the same time frame as Malachi. The particular event we are revisiting was reported by Ezra. A descendant of Aaron, Ezra was a priest who was granted permission by the Persian king, Artaxerxes, to lead a group of exiles back to Jerusalem. The king also gave Ezra the authority to teach the law of God to the exiles in Jerusalem.

Read Ezra 9:1–2. Describe the situation found here. What similarities do you see with Malachi 2?

Read Ezra 9:3–7 and 10:1. How did the family of God, as a whole, react when sin was discovered in their midst?

What do you think about the fact that the whole took responsibility for the sin of a few?

When God saved you, He saved you into His family. Though you are one member, God has uniquely joined you with other members to form a body, with Christ as head (1 Corinthians 12:12–27). If sin enters the body—even at one small point—the entire body is affected. Again, each of us is responsible *to* and *for* the entire body.

As we end today, contemplate the nature of the body of Christ. Did God give you any new insight?

Also consider the individual church body into which God has placed you. Can you identify any issues in your own life or that of the church body that are not glorifying to God?

DAY 5

No Compromise!

Ralph had been feeling fine except for a minor sore throat. Then one afternoon, he was hit with unbelievable tremors that sent him to the hospital emergency room. During examination, the medical staff noticed a red, fingertip-size spot on his left calf. Within minutes, it had grown to the size of a softball. The diagnosis was serious. Ralph had flesh-eating disease. Treatment was fast and aggressive. During emergency surgery, the doctor cut Ralph's leg from the top of his thigh down to his ankle to remove the diseased tissue. Nine days of strong antibiotics followed.

Necrotizing fasciitis, commonly know as flesh-eating disease, can be caused by a number of different bacteria, including group A streptococcus. The bacteria often enters the body at a weak point, the place of a minor injury, like a small cut or bruise. Infection then spreads rapidly through the layers of tissue. It can bring death in as little as 12 hours. This condition is fatal in about 20 to 30 percent of cases, but, thankfully, it is extremely rare.[6]

God worked through miraculous and medical means to save not only Ralph's leg but also his life. Ralph, now a pastor in Edmonton, was a seminary student and a member of my church in Alberta at the time of his illness. Ralph's doctors and nurses were all amazed at the speed of his recovery. Ralph unapologetically gave the glory to God.

Like flesh-eating disease, sin attacks us where we are vulnerable. It is easy to resist temptation in our strong areas; it is equally easy to compromise in our weak areas. Again, like this necrotizing fasciitis, compromise begins in just one small area. No big deal. But over time, if left untreated, compromise begins to work its way through the layers of our lives, destroying everything in its path. What's the cure for compromise? Cut it out. Get rid of it completely. The longer we wait, the more radical the necessary surgery becomes.

Read Malachi 2:10–16 (NIV, if possible). What similar phrases do you find in verses 10, 11, and 14?

Certain individuals and, therefore, the nation of Israel had broken their covenant of faith with God. They had compromised with the ways of the world around them. They had divorced the wives of their youth, married pagan women, and fallen into idolatry by following after the gods of their new pagan wives. God despised and denounced their behavior (v. 16) and then determined a course of action for them.

Reread Malachi 2:15–16. What two specific responses does God demand from those who have compromised their obedience and broken faith?

Twice, God specifically told the people to *"guard"* themselves in their spirits and *"not break faith"* (in other words, be obedient to the commands of the covenant). Malachi does not describe for us how the people responded to God's direction at this point. Instead, the prophet moves quickly on to another area of concern. However, let's return to the similar situation in Ezra—the one we looked at yesterday—to see how it was resolved.

Read Ezra 10:1–17.

This event serves as an excellent example of how God's people, individually and corporately, must deal with sin. Four distinct components can be seen in this passage:

1. **Recognition:** Sin in our own lives or in the life of the church must first be identified and acknowledged.
2. **Repentance:** Not only must we agree with God that our behavior is indeed sin, but we must also be grieved over it to the point of turning from it in disgust. The Greek word that is translated as "repent" in the New Testament is *metanoeo* (found in Matthew 3:2, Luke 5:32, and Acts 2:38, for example). *Strong's Greek and Hebrew Dictionary* defines it as "to change one's mind for better, heartily to amend with abhorrence of one's past sins."[7]
3. **Removal:** True repentance always leads us to rid our lives of the sin God has revealed to us. We do not delay. We obey quickly and completely. We must do whatever it takes to get rid of sin in our lives. In Matthew 5:28–30, Jesus made use of hyperbole to emphasize the seriousness of this issue. *"If your right eye causes you to sin, gouge it out and throw it away"* (v. 29).
4. **Restoration:** The presence of sin strains our relationships with God and other people, and the removal of sin brings restoration and renewal of those same relationships. Remember, sin will not sever the relationship between God and one of His children; since we did nothing to earn our salvation, we can do nothing to lose it. However, the continuing presence of sin in our lives does affect the quality of our relationship with God.

What evidence do you see in Ezra 10 for the presence of each of these four components?

Describe any other action you see in this passage that was significant in dealing with their sin.

Before we end today's lesson, let's take a closer look at God's command to guard ourselves. For our lives to be pleasing to God, we must strive to go beyond merely removing sin as we commit it. The treatment for flesh-eating disease is twofold: removal and protection. The diseased flesh is surgically removed, radically if necessary. Then the patient is inundated with strong antibiotics to protect him or her against a recurrence or new infection. Likewise, Christians must take measures to protect their lives from the possibility of sin and compromise.

The word translated as "guard" in Malachi 2:15–16 is the Hebrew word *shamar*. It is defined as "to be on one's guard, take heed, take care, beware."[8] This same Hebrew word is found five times in Deuteronomy 11. In that passage, Moses was preparing the nation of Israel to go into and take possession of the Promised Land. Moses encouraged them with the promised blessings of God if they were careful to be obedient, and he warned them about the discipline of God if they were not obedient. *Shamar* is found in verses 1, 8, 16, 22, and 32. Depending on your translation, it may appear as any of several related English words or phrases, such as *diligently keep, observe, obey, keep, carefully keep, take heed,* or *beware.*

Read Proverbs 4:20–27. In many versions of the Bible, *shamar*, found in verse 21, is translated as "keep." Based on this passage, describe how Christians should take protective action to guard themselves against or keep themselves from sin.

Reflect on your own life. In what areas do you need to be on your guard? What specific actions can you take to protect yourself from yielding to compromise and falling into sin?

Meditate on the following Scripture as you go on your way today.

Because we have these promises, dear friends, let us cleanse ourselves from everything that can defile our body or spirit. And let us work toward complete purity because we fear God.

—2 Corinthians 7:1 (NLT)

WEEK 6

GOD DEMONSTRATES HIS JUSTICE

Judge Judith Sheindlin has been deciding actual cases over the television airways since 1996. If you have a legal matter in which you cannot get justice, you may submit it through her Web site as a possible case for the show. She hears two cases daily before a large television audience.

One of Judge Judy's cases involved a lawsuit between a woman and her hairstylist. The woman claimed her recent bald spots were caused by the stylist's faulty application of hair extensions.[1] Judge Judy decided this case as she does most all cases—with "no-nonsense, hard-hitting decisiveness, combined with her biting wit," as one television critic describes her style.[2]

Something about all this seems to poke fun at our American justice system. The image of the dignified judge in a somber courtroom has been pushed to the background by the sharp-tongued judge whom all of America calls by her first name.

Hopefully, none of us will have to stand before Judge Judy while all of America watches. But there is one Judge we will all stand before. God is the ultimate and eternal Judge. His judgments are always just, and His decisions are always right.

DAY 1

The Certainty of God's Judgment

Criminals go free. The innocent are punished. The disadvantaged are abused. Have you ever wondered about the abundance of apparent injustice in the world? I have. Have you ever asked God why evil, at times, seems to prevail? I have. And so did the people in Malachi's day. Today we are going to explore God's answer to them.

Read Malachi 2:17 through 3:5. Now reread 2:17. Rephrase, in your own words, the people's accusations and questions that have "wearied" the Lord.

Remember, these are the same people who had offered blemished sacrifices, profaned the Lord's name, broken God's covenant, and compromised their obedience, leading them into idolatry. And then they accused God of loving evil and forsaking justice! Sometimes my children use a similar tactic when they are disobedient. They try to shift the focus off their own behavior by bringing up something they think is wrong with me. This tactic is an effort to avoid taking responsibility for their behavior. It rarely works with me, and it never works with God.

Read Romans 2:1–11. Using information from this passage, write a rebuttal to the people's accusations in Malachi 2:17. Include information like God's stance on evil and the certainty of coming judgment.

God is always and eternally just. It is His divine nature to be so. But God's timing for *when* He delivers His judgment is up to Him. Throughout Scripture, we see examples of immediate judgment, like when Achan took the plunder from Jericho (Joshua 7), and instances of judgment delayed until God's appointed time. But no matter the timing, judgment *will* come—if not in the course of history, then at the end of time at the final judgment. Romans 2 leaves no doubt that every person will stand before the judgment seat of God. Each will have to answer to the Creator for how he or she lived the life He gave. But what will this final judgment look like for believers?

Read Matthew 25:31–46. How will Jesus make a distinction between those who belong to Him and those who do not? What will be the eternal results for each group?

When Jesus returns, He will make a very clear distinction between persons who are saved and those who are lost. The word *sheep* is used often in the Scriptures as a symbolic term for believers. After giving the "sheep" the place of honor at His right hand, Jesus invites them to come receive the divine blessing of their eternal inheritance. The "goats" are sent away to eternal punishment. Jesus uses the difference in behavior between the sheep and the goats to explain His reason for the distinction. The sheep helped those in need; the goats did not. Yet the Scriptures are clear that salvation is not based on works, but on faith in Christ and His sacrificial death.

Michael J. Wilkins, in his commentary on Matthew, writes that the sheep's surprised reaction (vv. 38–39) to Jesus's praise is evidence "that these [the sheep's caring acts] were not intentional meritorious acts to gain access to the kingdom. Rather, these acts of mercy are evidences that the sheep belong to the kingdom."[3] Their acts, therefore, are the result of transformation by the Holy Spirit. The opposite is true of the goats. The lack of mercy is evidence that the Holy Spirit has not been active in their lives. They do not belong to God. Real faith will reveal itself in good works (James 2:14–18).

As we saw in Matthew 25, even believers will stand before the judgment seat of Christ. And remember that the heavenly Father does not have favorites:

> *And remember that the heavenly Father to whom you pray has no favorites when he judges. He will judge or reward you according to what you do. So you must live in reverent fear of him during your time as foreigners here on earth.*
>
> —1 Peter 1:17 (NLT)

While we *will* have to answer as to how we spent the life God gave us, we *will not* have to fear eternal condemnation.

Read Romans 8:1–4. Why will believers not have to face God's condemnation?

Read 1 John 4:13–21. According to this passage, what evidence in the lives of believers will demonstrate that they belong to God?

When we give our lives to God, we enter into a relationship of love. Once we are within this relationship, the only way we can experience all the blessings God has for His children is if we appropriately fear Him. Godly fear brings us to complete obedience. Complete obedience makes us more like Christ. Christlikeness makes God's love more and more complete within us. This love, then, casts out the fear of His judgment, but does not cast off the proper fear of God.

As previously discussed, Christians need to find in their relationship with God the position of proper tension of seeing God as both Father and Master. This passage we just read in 1 John is very helpful in understanding what it means for believers to fear God, but 1 John 4:18 stresses that believers do not need to fear God's judgment.

Gary Burge elaborates in his commentary on the Letters of John: "There can be no apprehensiveness or fear of God when we fully comprehend his love. Fear and love are mutually exclusive. To fear the character of God or to fear the final judgment paralyzes us."[4] Yet Burge readily agrees that we believers must consider more than just God's love. If we do not, we run the risk of "losing profound respect for him, because we have made him too personal, too approachable."[5] As a comparison with God's position of authority in our lives, Burge provides the example of an absolute monarch with great power. This monarch has the potential to be our greatest benefactor or greatest enemy. Burge wants believers to feel a tension when they consider the character of God. He wants them "to feel fear, awe, privilege, and blessing—all at the same moment."[6]

Clearly, those of us who are in a love relationship with God need not fear condemnation at the time of His judgment. Like the sheep in Matthew 25, we will receive our eternal inheritance. Yet we should contemplate the seriousness and finality of God's judgment.

The fierce certainty of God's impending judgment should deeply affect the lives of believers. Second Peter 3 emphasizes that the certainty of God's judgment should be an impetus for holy living (vv. 11–14). Even though eternity for believers is secure through their relationship with Jesus, the fact that God will one day sit in supreme and final judgment over the world and everyone in it should cause believers to bend their wills to His in complete obedience. Additionally, Peter makes it clear that God does not want any person to perish (v. 9). This should move believers to introduce others to Jesus, the only Way of salvation (John 14:6).

❱✦ **Before we end today, list below the names of people you know who need to be introduced to Jesus.**

🐦 **Without a relationship with Jesus, these people have every reason to fear God's final judgment. Will you commit to pray for their salvation? Will you ask God to show you how you can be a witness to them? Are you willing to obey His direction?**

Day 2

God's Purification of His Children

Throughout this study, we have emphasized the fact that God calls believers to be holy. *"For he chose us in him before the creation of the world to be holy and blameless in his sight"* (Ephesians 1:4). *"But just as he who called you is holy, so be holy in all you do; for it is written: 'Be holy, because I am holy'"* (1 Peter 1:15–16). God's priority for our lives is holiness. He cares more about our character being conformed to the image of Christ than He does about our physical comfort or earthly success (2 Corinthians 4:7–18). Therefore, for those of us who are believers, God will work to purify our lives. His Spirit within us constantly works to shape and mold us to be more like Him (2 Corinthians 3:16–18).

God chose Israel to be a holy nation. Israel was set apart for the purpose of reflecting God to a lost world. Unfortunately, during the time of Malachi, Israel was reflecting the world and its ways, not God and His holiness. In the first two chapters of Malachi, God, through the prophet, denounced many specific sins of Israel. As we begin chapter 3, God announces His intentions to purify the nation.

Read Malachi 3:1–5.

Sin was prevalent in Israel during Malachi's time. This is emphasized by the people's question in Malachi 2:17: *"Where is the God of justice?"* God's response in Malachi 3:1–5 leaves no room for doubt. The Lord God *is* coming as judge, and He *is* bringing justice. Yet God's messenger must prepare the way first. In the New Testament, Jesus quoted Malachi 3:1 and identified this messenger as John the Baptist (Matthew 11:10;

Luke 7:27). However, the *"messenger of the covenant"* (mentioned later in Malachi 3:1) is Christ. His coming marked the beginning of God's judgment on the godless members of God's covenant nation. His coming also brought God's New Covenant to the world. This covenant was not written on tablets of stone, but on the hearts of men (Hebrews 8:10). Were they ready?

Read Matthew 3:1–2. What did John urge the people to do and why?

Read Matthew 3:5–12. What was the difference between the baptism by John and the baptism by Jesus?

Apply John's message to the people in Malachi. What did the people need to do before God came to them as judge?

Yes, God, who is just, was coming to judge sinful Israel. Yet God, who is merciful, would give them the opportunity to repent. I find it ironic that the people were clamoring for God's justice when they themselves were steeped in sin. I can imagine them looking at the disobedience of those around them, wondering when God would intervene and put a stop to it. They wanted God to judge their neighbors, but I doubt they wanted God to bring justice to their own houses. Malachi assured them that the God of justice they were looking for was indeed coming (Malachi 3:1). Then he added, *"But who will be able to endure it when he comes? Who will be able to stand and face him when he appears?"* (Malachi 3:2 NLT).

Reread Malachi 3:1–5. According to this passage, when the Lord comes as judge, what actions of judgment will He take? Look for verbs that describe what He will do.

What will be the positive results?

Take another look at verse 5. What was the root cause for the sin in Israel? (*Hint:* The Hebrew word *yare'* (fear) is found in the latter part of the verse. For more information on its definition, review language notes in the week 1, day 3 study.)

God wants His children to be holy. Therefore, He must identify and discipline blatant disobedience (v. 5); He must cleanse sinful attitudes and behavior (vv. 2 and 3); and He must purify and refine lives so they will reflect Him (vv. 3 and 4). We are going to spend the last three days of this week focusing on God's activity of justice in our lives.

Look up the following Scripture passages, and identify each specific work or activity of God (in any of His persons: Father, Son, or Holy Spirit) that is evident in the lives of believers. What is the purpose of the work or activity?

- **Revelation 3:19**

- **2 Corinthians 7:1** (**Note:** While this verse is stated as a command to believers, we know that only the Holy Spirit can accomplish the task. However, we must cooperate by obediently yielding our lives to His work within us. Also note that the Greek noun *phobos*, which means "fear, dread, terror; that which strikes terror; reverence for one's husband,"[7] is found at the end of this verse. For the definition of the verb *phobeo*, refer to the week 4, day 4 lesson.)

- **2 Timothy 1:8–9a**

I see described in the New Testament three different ways that God's Holy Spirit works in the lives of those of us who are believers to move us toward holiness. While the different ways are not mutually exclusive, I do believe that God does use these three ways progressively in our lives to bring spiritual maturity.

1. **Disciplining:** God uses correction and training to bring those of us who are His children to repentance and cleanse us from sinful

behavior, including what we do wrong as well as right things we do not do. We will focus on this area of God's justice tomorrow.

2. **Refining/Purifying:** This deeper area of "holiness training" goes beyond our surface behavior. With this type training, God shapes and molds our character, roots out our fleshly desires, and reforms sinful attitudes that serve as the basis for our behavior. The Holy Spirit works to purify and refine them so we will be clean and pliable for the Master's use. This will be our topic for day 4 of this week.

3. **Sharing in Christ's suffering:** As we mature spiritually (move toward holiness), our lives of obedience and self-denial become more and more offensive to the world. The Bible says that if we suffer persecution because we are a Christian, then we are sharing in the sufferings of Christ Himself (1 Peter 4:12–16). Both Paul and Peter considered this kind of suffering a privilege. On day 5 of this week, we will consider the privilege of sharing in Christ's sufferings and how God uses it to move us even closer toward holiness.

As we end today's study, spend some time *preparing the way* for God to do a work in your heart during the rest of this week. Apply John the Baptist's message to your own life. What work is the Holy Spirit doing in your life now? Are you willing to yield your life to His further discipline and refinement so you can experience the joy of sharing in Christ's sufferings?

DAY 3

God's Discipline of His Children

I love my dad. And I have never doubted his love for me. I know he always wants what is best for me. As a father, his patience runs very deep. (Though I must say, he needed more patience with my brother, than with me.) Yet when I was growing up, the huge amount of love and respect I felt for him was tinged with an element of fear. Why? Because I understood that he had certain expectations for my behavior, and that if I rebelliously went against those expectations, there would be consequences.

He loved me enough to discipline me when I needed it. Sometimes his discipline was for the purpose of correcting wrong behavior. For example, if

I talked back to Mom, then I lost my telephone privileges. That was a tough one.

Sometimes Dad's discipline was for the purpose of teaching me something I did not already know but needed to know to succeed in life. For instance, Dad determined I would be the one in the family who regularly raked the pine straw in the yard. Lest you think this was a simple chore, you need to know that on my parents' half-acre lot are 24 pine trees.

As an adolescent, I saw no point in this task. What difference did it make that the grass was covered with pine needles? Even if I did rake, the grass would soon be covered again. Yet I grudgingly obeyed. Now that I am a parent myself, I can appreciate Dad's training. I learned that every member of the family needs to help. I learned to persevere through unpleasant, but necessary tasks. I learned that a job done well brings pleasurable results.

God also disciplines His children. As we discussed on day 1 of this week, as believers, we do not have to fear eternal judgment, but we can expect God's discipline. If we are disobedient, we can expect temporal judgment in the form of discipline. Let's look at two biblical examples of temporal judgment—one from the Old Testament and one from the New Testament.

Read 2 Samuel 12:7–14. What was David's sin? How did God discipline David for his sin?

Did David repent? What evidence do you see that God's judgment of discipline on David was only temporal and not eternal?

Read 1 Corinthians 11:27–32. What was the sin of some of the Corinthian believers (vv. 17–22)?

How did God discipline them? How could they have avoided God's discipline (vv. 28, 31)?

God's discipline of believers is only temporal judgment. It does not dictate or affect our eternal destination. With our salvation being based solely on receiving what Christ did on our behalf, we cannot be good enough to earn our salvation, and we cannot be bad enough to lose it. We, as believers, are judged and disciplined, but not condemned:

> *When we are judged by the Lord, we are being disciplined so that we will not be condemned with the world.*
>
> —1 Corinthians 11:32

Craig Blomberg, in discussion of 1 Corinthians 11 in his commentary on that book of the Bible, elaborates: "Paul ends on a somewhat upbeat note by reminding his readers that even those who have died for their actions are not damned.... Rather God disciplines those he loves to protect them from further damaging themselves or others."[8]

Think of times in your life that God used discipline to correct sinful behavior. Can you see ways that His discipline protected you or others around you? If so, will you thank God for His hand of discipline?

Moses told the Israelites that God disciplines His people like a father disciplines his son (Deuteronomy 8:5). According to Proverbs 3:11–12, God disciplines those He loves. Paul told the Corinthian church that God disciplined them for their own good (1 Corinthians 11:32). The author of Hebrews gives us even further insight into God's discipline.

Read Hebrews 12:7–11, and review the language notes to the right. Take note of the two levels of discipline found in the definition of *paideuo*. The second level is what is expressed in Hebrews 12.

Language Notes

Hebrews 12:7–11

English: **discipline/chastise**
Greek: ***paideuo***
Definition:
- to train children—to be instructed or taught or learn; to cause one to learn
- to chastise—to chastise or castigate with words, to correct; of those who are molding the character of others by reproof and admonition

---

Can you think of a time God used His discipline to train you or teach you right behavior not yet exhibited in your life?

Reread Hebrews 12:7–11. What does God's discipline in your life prove?

How should we respond to God's discipline?

According to this passage, what is the purpose of God's discipline?

We don't seem to hear much about God's discipline in our churches today. I believe that is partly because we highlight what we consider to be God's more positive attributes, like mercy, grace, and love, in order to make our message more palatable to a wider audience. Paul spoke about this in 2 Timothy 4:3: *"For the time will come when men will not put up with sound doctrine. Instead, to suit their own desires, they will gather around them a great number of teachers to say what their itching ears want to hear."*

As we close today, please contemplate the following quote:

Many Christians seem to disregard the prospect of God's discipline. They apparently don't believe that stubborn and persistent continuance in sin will invoke God's fatherly displeasure. They mistake God's grace for a license to live as they please, on the assumption that God's forgiveness is automatic and unconditional....

These people apparently have no fear of God's discipline. They're strangers to the idea of living their lives in reverent fear.

And what about us?... Anytime we sin with the thought lurking in the back of our minds that God will forgive us, we aren't living in the fear of God.[9]

—Jerry Bridges, *The Joy of Fearing God*

🕊 **Have you ever taken advantage of God's grace? Can you identify with anything in the statement above?**

🕊 **Has your view of God's discipline changed during the course of this study? If so, how?**

DAY 4

God's Refining of Those Who Fear Him

God says He will purify His children by refining them like silver. I didn't know anything about silver refining, so I did a little research on smelting, the process that extracts metal from its ore. I found that the steps for this original refining process are very relevant to our study today.

The process begins with a quantity of silver ore, which is basically rock with a little silver in it. The ore is first crushed to a powder, then it is washed to dissolve many unwelcome contaminants. This cycle is repeated until the water is clear.

Next, the ore is placed in a furnace with lead or charcoal. The furnace is heated to an extremely high temperature (between 1450°C–2000°C) to melt everything—additional contaminates, the lead, and the silver within the ore. The lead, acting as a scavenger, adheres to the silver. Then the metals, which are heavier than the contaminates, sink to the bottom of the furnace. The contaminates, or slag, can then be drained off the top.

After most of the slag is removed, the metals in the bottom of the furnace are tapped and poured into a mold. This mixture of lead and silver must be heated again to separate the metals. This time the furnace is heated to a temperature that is sufficient to melt the lead, but not the silver (about 900°C). When the lead is drained, what remains is essentially pure silver. Even though this is an extremely simplified version of the smelting process, it helped me to appreciate how much time and work goes into the refining of even one ounce of silver.

God refines His people like silver, and His refining process in the life of a believer is not easy: beginning with just an ordinary lump of hard rock, crush and wash and wash again, fire and heat, melt and separate, drain and mold, heat again, and shape. The result is a pure product that the Master Smelter can use in any way He chooses. Are you willing? Then ask God to turn up the heat!

Read Malachi 3:2–4. As a review of our study on day 2 of this week, list the actions of judgment God will take in the lives of His people.

Use a dictionary to define the following:
- **Refine**
- **Purify**

Using these definitions and the Malachi passage, write in your own words what God wants to do in the life of every believer.

What does the refining process look like in the life of a believer? In Malachi, God uses the refining of silver as an analogy. And in the New Testament, Peter compares the refining of precious metals to the strengthening of our faith. Read the following passage from the New Living Translation:

So be truly glad! There is wonderful joy ahead, even though it is necessary for you to endure many trials for a while. These trials are only to test your faith, to show that it is strong and pure. It is being tested as fire tests and purifies gold—and your faith is far more precious to God than mere gold. So if your faith remains strong after being tried by fiery trials, it will bring you much

---

Language Notes

1 Peter 1:6

English: **trials/temptations**
Greek: *peirasmos*
Definition: the trial of man's fidelity, integrity, virtue, and constancy through:
- an enticement to sin, temptation, whether arising from the desires or from the outward circumstances
- an internal temptation to sin
- of the condition of things, or a mental state, by which we are enticed to sin, or to a lapse from the faith and holiness
- adversity, affliction, trouble; sent by God and serving to test or prove one's character, faith, holiness

praise and glory and honor on the day when Jesus Christ is revealed to the whole world.

—1 Peter 1:6–7 (NLT)

Based on this passage, what does God use to refine our faith? What are the results?

Many fiery trials! The refining process sounds painful, doesn't it? Let's look at the language notes on the previous page to gain some insight on the *"fiery trials"* that God uses to refine believers.

First of all, notice that the definition includes the element of being tempted to sin. Although this element is not present in 1 Peter 1:6, our faith *is* tested when we experience temptation. For this aspect of the use of *peirasmos*, see Matthew 6:13 and James 1:12. Some of these temptations come from outside sources and some come from our own fleshly desires and weaknesses.

Let's look further into the definition of *peirasmos*. We see that some fiery trials are circumstantial. God purifies our faith and character by allowing us to experience adversity, affliction, and trouble through the normal course of life.

How do you think our faith can be refined by facing temptation?

How do you think our faith can be refined by experiencing adversity?

✍ Describe how God has used temptation and adversity in your own life to refine your faith.

The refining process is painful but necessary. Refining and purifying penetrates below the surface features of our lives. God must go beyond disciplining our outward behavior and get to the root of any problems. He works through temptation and adversity to reveal what is in our hearts and minds. James talks about this refining work of trials and the purpose of it.

Read James 1:2–4. According to this passage, what is the result in believers' lives when they persevere through fiery trials?

Why is silver refined? To rid it of contaminates so it will be useful. Refined silver is in high demand today because of its unique properties. Besides being beautiful, silver is strong, malleable, and ductile. The ability to be flattened, stretched, hammered, and shaped without breaking and the characteristic of being an excellent conductor of heat and electricity make silver an indispensable component in many products, from batteries and circuit breakers to microwaves and computers. But its value doesn't end there. Silver also has the ability to kill bacteria and purify water. Many people groups, from the Phoenicians to the American pioneers, put silver in their water containers to keep the water pure and clean. Silver is being used increasingly today for swimming pool systems and drinking water purifiers. As a bactericide, silver has been used over the centuries and is continuing to be used to prevent or treat a wide range of diseases and infections.[10]

Consider these properties of silver as part of the analogy. How could these properties be exhibited in the life of a refined believer?

Before we end today, I want us to consider one more property of silver. Silver is the best-known reflector of visible light. In fact, a silver refiner knows that his metal is pure when he can see his own image reflected in the mirrorlike surface of the metal.[11]

Please read 2 Corinthians 3:17–18 from the New Living Translation:

Now, the Lord is the Spirit, and wherever the Spirit of the Lord is, he gives freedom. And all of us have had that veil removed so that we can be mirrors that brightly reflect the glory of the Lord. And as the Spirit of the Lord works within us, we become more and more like him and reflect his glory even more.

—2 Corinthians 3:17–18 (NLT)

✎ **Based on what we have studied today, why do you think God wants to purify you like silver? Are you willing to give Him access to do just that?**

DAY 5

Identification with Christ's Sufferings

The story of Stephen, the first Christian martyr, is recorded in Acts 7. His stoning was just the beginning of Christian suffering. From the time of Stephen, through the centuries, and continuing today, Christians have been suffering and dying for their faith.

While we may be saddened when we hear news about the persecution of Christians around the world, we are probably not surprised. We may even expect it. But do you expect it in your own city, in your own life? Yes, there have been isolated events in America, but have you really thought you would—or even *should*—experience persecution?

Brian Bosma, who was elected speaker of the Indiana House of Representatives in November 2004, knows what it's like to face persecution because of his faith—persecution here in America, by Americans. Bosma's stand on prayer initiated the trouble. The Indiana Civil Liberties Union (ICLU) filed a lawsuit in June 2005 against Bosma for the use of the name of Jesus in opening prayers for daily sessions of the Indiana House. Prayer itself is not the issue. The Indiana House of Representatives has been opening its sessions with prayer since 1826. However, the ICLU claims that the use of the name of Jesus in prayers to open the House's daily sessions is unconstitutional. Individual plaintiffs have said that such prayers are offensive to people who are not Christians and the practice creates a policy of exclusion.[12] So Bosma has been targeted in one of many attempts to stop Christians in America from publicly testifying to our Lord and Savior. This reminds me of an incident reported in the New Testament.

Read Acts 5:40–41. Scan the passage before verse 40 to get the context. Why were the apostles beaten?

How did the apostles regard the beating, and how did they respond?

This persecution probably did not come as a surprise to the apostles. Jesus had told them it would come. The night of His betrayal just before His arrest, Jesus spent the evening preparing the apostles for what was in store for them, what they could expect.

Read John 15:18–21. Why does the world (those not belonging to Christ) hate and persecute true followers of Christ?

Those who followed the ways of the world hated Jesus because His *righteousness* revealed their *sin* (John 7:7). If we are living lives that reveal the righteousness of Christ (holiness), the world will hate us for the same reason—our lives expose the sin of the world. When we are like Christ, or Christlike, the world will respond with persecution because those in the world see us as a threat to the status quo.

A number of years ago, God impressed me with the sad truth that my life did not draw much, if any, ridicule, scorn, or persecution from the world. What was the reason? I was not enough like Christ to be any threat to the world and its ways.

What about you? Have you ever had to endure suffering because you bear the name of Christ? Keep in mind, we must not confuse experiencing the consequences of sin or even the common trials of life with suffering for the name of Christ. This latter kind of suffering is a result of a believer's self-denial and obedience to the will of God. The Scriptures make a clear distinction.

Read 1 Peter 4:12–19. What is distinct about suffering for the name of Christ compared with other kinds of suffering?

How should we react when we share in the sufferings of Christ? (Don't miss the truths in verse 19.)

Read 1 Peter 4:1–2. This passage begins with the word therefore. Near the end of 1 Peter 3, we are reminded that our salvation was made possible through the suffering of Christ. How, therefore, should we live in response?

How does God use suffering in the lives of His children?

Based on what you discovered in this passage and others in today's lesson, write a summary statement about sharing in the sufferings of Christ.

Wow! How contrary to the world's thinking! Sharing in the sufferings of Christ is not something we should avoid. It is something we should embrace. Paul eagerly desired to share in Christ's sufferings so he could know Christ more (Philippians 3:7–10). God also uses the suffering in our lives that naturally comes as a result of our complete obedience to Him to further refine our faith (2 Corinthians 4:7–10). These passages and others teach that sharing in the sufferings of Christ is part of God's will for the life of a believer.

What real and eternal purpose can God possibly find in allowing His children to suffer persecution and even martyrdom? Josef Tson, president of the Romanian Missionary Society, answers this very question in his book *Suffering, Martyrdom and Rewards in Heaven.* Tson says that the suffering and death of Christ reveals that God uses this kind of self-sacrifice to deal with mankind's rebellion and sin. When believers, in the name of Christ, face persecution or even death with the grace of God, it is a powerful testimony to the unbeliever. Tson elaborates:

> When the ambassador of Christ speaks the truth in love, and meets death with joy, a strange miracle occurs: the eyes of unbelievers are opened, they are enabled to see the truth of God, and this leads them to believe in the gospel. Ever since the centurion's eyes were opened at Calvary, ever since he believed that Jesus was the Son of God *because* he had

seen the manner of His death (Mark 15:39), thousands and thousands of Christian martyrdoms over the centuries have produced the same results.[13]

—Josef Tson, *Suffering, Martyrdom and Rewards in Heaven*

When believers endure persecution with the same attitude that Jesus had, God is glorified and the hearts of unbelievers are turned to Christ. Hallelujah! If God counts me worthy to share in the sufferings of Christ, it will be a privilege and a blessing!

God wants to use our lives as a testimony to Christ in this world. He purposed the same for the nation of Israel. But in the days of Malachi, the lives of the people were not fit for God's use. Through His prophet, God called them to repent and to prepare for the coming of Christ (*"the messenger of the covenant"*), who would bring God's justice to Israel. This week we considered the role of God's justice in our own lives. We saw how God uses discipline and refining to purify us and move us toward holiness. Today, we considered how God uses persecution in the lives of His children to bring glory to Himself.

Have you ever shared in the sufferings of Christ? If so, when and how? How did you respond? What was the result?

Do you recognize any areas of your life in which you have been less than completely obedient to God because you were afraid of how the world might react? If so, are you willing to submit them to God now and trust in His divine purposes? Write a prayer of response to God below.

WEEK 7

GOD DEPLORES "FEARLESS" DETOURS

An enormous amount of road construction is taking place in my city. I never know what overpass or main thoroughfare has been closed from one day to the next. Motorists constantly have to make detours. Although these detours increase the travel time to my destination, I can still usually get where I need to go.

While road detours are annoying, they are not hazardous to our spiritual well-being. However, spiritual detours can have eternal consequences. When God established the nation of Israel, He called them to follow after Him in faithful obedience. But throughout its history, Israel took one detour after another. Over and over, they left God's path and followed their own way. The Book of Malachi is a record of such a detour. Because they didn't fear God, the people had left His straight-and-narrow way and turned down a road of their own construction (Malachi 3:5).

This week we will study God's call to Israel to repent, turn around, and get back on the right road. He issues the same call to His children today. Every detour, no matter how small, will take us further and further away from God. I pray that each of us will heed His call to return.

DAY 1

The Unchanging God

I went into my favorite superstore recently to pick up a few items I needed for dinner. I was in a hurry, so I headed straight to the spot where I knew the rice would be. But it wasn't there. I decided to get my second item and look for the rice after that. I knew the canned soup would be two rows back at the opposite end, so I hustled over. No soup. OK, the milk *had* to be where I saw it last, I thought; so I moved on to the cooler at the back of the store. Orange juice. About that time, an employee sauntered by. When questioned, she readily admitted, "Oh, yes. We moved around a lot of things. We wanted to make them easier to find."

Sometimes it seems like the only thing we can depend on is change. Although the location of long-grain rice in the grocery store does not drastically affect my life, the dependability of other things does. For instance, my family and I depend on the regularity of my husband's paycheck to keep a roof over our heads and food in our stomachs.

🖎 **Think about the people and things you depend on. Fill out table 7 according to the headings.**

Table 7. People and things I count on

PEOPLE/ THINGS I DEPEND ON	WHAT THEY PROVIDE IN MY LIFE	THE CHANCE OF THEM BEING UNDEPENDABLE	HOW MY LIFE WOULD BE AFFECTED

No matter how dependable a person or provision is in your life, a chance of change always exists. Only one being—God—is eternally unchangeable and completely dependable. This truth about God should affect how we relate to Him and should impact every area of our lives. Today we are going to celebrate the fact that our God does not change!

Read Malachi 3:6–12, our passage for this week of study. Now reread verse 6, our focus for today. What does God not ever do?

Review language notes on the right. Considering the definitions of the Hebrew words *shanah* and *lo'* found in Malachi 3:6, write a true statement about the dependability of God's unchanging nature.

Language Notes

Malachi 3:6

English: **change**
Hebrew: *shanah*
Definition: change, alter, disguise, double, or pervert

English: **not**
Hebrew: *lo'* (adjective)
Definition: particle of negation (*Note:* When used with a verb like *shanah*, it implies absolute prohibition.)

Read Psalm 89:30–34. The Hebrew word *shanah* (change or alter) is found in verse 34. Compare this passage with Malachi 3:1–7. Complete table 8 by listing Israel's behavior and God's response to their behavior.

Table 8. God's response to Israel's behavior

ISRAEL'S BEHAVIOR	GOD'S RESPONSE

Based on table 8, what conclusions can you draw about God and His unchanging nature?

God reminded the Israelites that they were descendants of Jacob—the same Jacob He chose to love (Malachi 1:2–3). God's love and unchanging nature work together to reveal His faithfulness to His people.

Although Psalm 89 refers to David and his sons, the truths found in this psalm are still applicable. God's faithfulness does not depend on how I treat Him. God is faithful because He has always been faithful and will always be faithful. I can depend on the unchanging nature of God. The author of Hebrews expressed this thought beautifully about God the Son: *"Jesus Christ is the same yesterday and today and forever"* (Hebrews 13:8).

What do you find comforting about this truth in Hebrews 13:8?

From that thought, the author of Hebrews moved immediately on to this statement: *"Do not be carried away by all kinds of strange teachings"* (Hebrews 13:9). Because Jesus never changes, His teachings never change. George Guthrie, in his *Hebrews* commentary, wrote, "Changes in the winds of social and cultural thought do not change God's covenant or his moral requirements."[1] Unlike our standards, God's standards do not change.

Let's make some practical application of this truth. Think about behaviors and attitudes that are morally acceptable by today's standards but fall short of God's unchanging standards. I have listed a few categories to get you started. Feel free to add other categories as you think of them. List example behaviors and attitudes with each category.

- **Business and work life**
- **Relationships with spouse, parents, children, and friends**
- **Sexual activity**
- **Moral and ethical conduct**
- **Other**

🔖 Now consider your own relationship with God. Do your standards for the relationship, such as submission and obedience, meet God's standards? If not, what adjustments do you need to make?

Because God does not change, His expectations for His children are the same today as they were in the time of Malachi. Because God does not change, His love and faithfulness are the same today as they were in Malachi's day.

As we close today, read Psalm 102:25–27.

🔖 Rejoice in the truth that our God does not "change, alter, disguise, double, or pervert" (*shanah*). Write a prayer of thanksgiving and commitment to our unchangeable God.

DAY 2

God's Call to Return

My son, Mark, played soccer for the first time when he was four or five. Once during the third game of that first season, Mark got control of the ball. He broke away from the pack. He dribbled the ball downfield with his eye on the goal. One problem. He was headed in the wrong direction. "Mark, wrong way! Turn around!" my husband and I screamed, trying to get his attention. But it was no use. Triumphantly, he scored for the other team.

This event has become one of those stories that families tell again and again over the years. It's a story that always brings a chuckle. But it reminds me of how we sometimes behave in our relationship with God. Sometimes Christians break away from a close walk with God. We may take off in the opposite direction, headed toward our own goals and desires. God calls to us to turn around, come back. But we don't always heed His voice.

Please read Malachi 3:6–7. Summarize these two verses in your own words.

Read Malachi 3:5. This verse gives examples of specific sins that illustrate Israel had turned away from God's decrees.

According to the latter part of this verse, why did Israel turn away from God and turn toward sin?

God's people had turned away from Him and His decrees and had begun to indulge in sinful behavior because they had lost their fear of God! (*Note: Yare'*, the Hebrew word for "fear," is found in verse 5.) Henry Blackaby discusses this in his book *Holiness:* "When there is no fear of God, there is no fear of sin."[2] Because Malachi's audience did not fear God, they did not fear sin and its consequences. They did not believe that God would judge their disobedience. The people's statement and question to God in Malachi 2:17 are evidence of this: "*'All who do evil are good in the eyes of the LORD, and he is pleased with them' or 'Where is the God of justice?'*" Blackaby comments further on the loss of the fear of God:

> If you lose the fear of God, there is nothing to restrain you. Many do not believe God sees them and do not believe He is aware of the condition of their hearts. They think that if He sees them and does not stop them, that it is okay. But He does see you and may not stop you, and it is *not* okay.[3]
>
> —Henry Blackaby, *Holiness*

Read Proverbs 3:7, and, in light of that verse, read Malachi 3:5, 7. According to these verses, what behavior does God want from His people? (*Note: Yare'*, the Hebrew word for "fear," is found in both Proverbs 3:7 and Malachi 3:5. The Hebrew word *cuwr*, meaning "shun" or "turned away," is found in both Proverbs 3:7 and Malachi 3:7.)

Unfortunately, how do His people often behave?

What do you think the following statement from Proverbs 3:7 means: "*Do not be wise in your own eyes*"?

Christians are not perfect. Until we reach heaven, we will from time to time disobey God and do what is wise in our own eyes. But have you ever in your Christian life spent a period of time running in the wrong direction?

A number of years ago, I spent a season of about six months facing away from God. I was not participating in any morally wrong behavior. But due to some difficult circumstances, I became completely focused on myself. I turned away from spending time with God, listening to His voice, and obeying Him. I even heard Him calling me to return, come back, but I consciously ignored Him. After wallowing in self-pity for a while, I realized that I had turned away from the One who could really help. When I heeded His call to return, He was waiting with open arms.

Has there ever been a time, perhaps even now, when you turned away from God? If so, what brought you to that point? If you are there now, do you wonder how to get back?

Read Malachi 3:7. What is God's direction for those who have turned away? What promise does He make?

"*Return.*" God does not give up on those who have turned away. He calls them back and promises to be waiting. But what does it mean to return to God after having turned away? The Hebrew word *shuwb* is translated as "return." It implies a 180-degree turn. In the *Theological Wordbook of the Old Testament*, the verb *shûb [shuwb]* is described as combining two requisites for repentance: to turn *from* evil and to turn *to* the good. This definition highlights the believer's responsibility in the process of repentance or returning.[4]

Returning is all about repentance. No matter how long or for what reason a person turns away from God, turning away is sin. Sin does not sever a believer's relationship with God, but it does strain it—significantly. The relationship needs to be renewed, revived. Sin requires genuine repentance. Repentance is the beginning of revival in a believer's relationship with God.

> **End your study time today by reflecting on the quality of your relationship with God. Does the relationship need revival? If so, ask God to start showing you how you may have turned away from Him.**

DAY 3

Robbers of God

About ten years ago, one of my credit cards was stolen. Before I even realized it was missing, the thief had a great time at an upscale department store. I was so angry. "How dare that person? The card was not his or hers to use. I have been wronged!" All these thoughts and more went through my mind. If you have ever been robbed, you probably experienced a similar reaction. But have you ever been the thief?

Read Malachi 3:6–12. What did God accuse the people of in verse 8?

Yesterday we considered God's call to return. Israel had turned away from God and turned to sin because they did not fear Him. In Malachi 3:5, God listed several specific sins that were evidence of their lack of fear. Then in verse 8, God gave another glaring example. The people were not giving their tithes and offerings to provide for the House of God.

The concept of the tithe in the Scriptures is as old as Abraham (Genesis 14:17–20). The Hebrew word translated as "tithe" is *ma'aser. Ma'aser* means a "tenth" or "payment of a tenth part." *Terumah,* translated as "offerings," refers to gifts that the people gave voluntarily, above their tithe, perhaps for a special purpose.[5] To help us understand tithing, let's take a look at God's instruction given to the nation of Israel in regard to the tithe.

Read Leviticus 27:30–34. What were the people commanded to tithe?

Read Numbers 18:21–29. Where did the people's tithes go? Why?

What was God's command to the Levites regarding the tithe? What was it used for?

> *"You must set aside a tithe of your crops—one-tenth of all the crops you harvest each year. Bring this tithe to the place the LORD your God chooses for his name to be honored, and eat it there in his presence. This applies to your tithes of grain, new wine, olive oil, and the firstborn males of your flocks and herds. The purpose of tithing is to teach you always to fear the LORD your God."*
>
> —Deuteronomy 14:22–23 (NLT)

According to this passage from Deuteronomy, what does God want to teach His people through the act of tithing?

How do you think God could use this act of obedience to teach us this particular lesson?

Read the following passages, and record the truths you find.
- Psalm 24:1
- 1 Timothy 6:17
- James 1:17

Do these passages give you any additional insight on what God wants to teach us through tithing? If so, what is it?

God promised the people He would pour out a blessing on them if they brought Him the whole tithe. I have often heard this passage incorrectly claimed as a promise that God will financially bless those who tithe. While God's blessing in the lives of His children may include wealth, it has a much greater scope than finances.

The Hebrew word for *"blessing"* in Malachi 3:10 is the same word used in Deuteronomy 28:2 to describe what God will do for Israel if the people are obedient to His commands. These blessings, detailed in the verses that follow verse 2, include various good things, like blessed children, fertile livestock and fields, protection from enemies, and rain at the proper time. God has a storehouse of abundance that is not limited to money. Therefore, the expectation for God to bless us financially is not the basis for our tithing.

Now let's consider how these truths apply to us, as New Covenant believers. Remember, as Christians under the New Covenant, we may not be bound to the letter of the law, but the greater spirit of the law should be written on our hearts and minds (2 Corinthians 3:6; Hebrews 10:16).

Read 1 Corinthians 9:11–14. What principles for giving are found here?

Read 2 Corinthians 9:6–13. Based on this passage, describe the proper motivation and attitude for giving.

In what ways does God promise to bless the giver?

Name at least three reasons that God blesses the giver. Particularly note verses 8*b* and 11.

This passage in 2 Corinthians contains some important truths. First, God does not bless a giver when the giver's motivation is to receive a blessing. Second, God's blessing in a believer's life is not necessarily of a material nature. Scott Hafemann, in his *2 Corinthians* commentary, explains: "God's promise in 2 Corinthians 9:10 is not to make his people rich but to use them as instruments of his presence for the salvation of others."[6]

Everything we have belongs to God because it came from Him. God wants to use our lives as channels of blessing to reach a lost world for Christ. He blesses us with finances, resources, time, and talents. His desire is that we use them for His glory. Let's get really personal as we close today.

🕊 **List the blessings of God in your life. Be sure to include finances, resources, time, and talents.**

🕊 **Are you allowing God to use these in your life to bless those around you? How?**

🕊 **Are you stealing or have you ever stolen from God?**

Day 4

Repentance, the First Step Toward Fear

We have talked all week about the need for God's people to return to Him. In the Book of Malachi, God held up the sinful life of His people as evidence that they had turned away from Him because they did not fear Him. We cannot just study Malachi, open our minds, and drop in the facts. We must allow God to use the truths He shows us to discipline us and refine our lives for His use (James 1:22–25).

We have learned a direct connection exists between our obedience to God and our fear of Him. What does our life reveal about our level of awe, respect, and honor for God? Today we are going to take a hard look at ourselves.

Read Galatians 5:16–26.

In this passage, Paul is admonishing the Christians in the Roman province of Galatia. The Galatians were worldly; their lives did not reflect Christ.

Today, almost 2,000 years later, Christians are still fighting the same battle with our own fleshly desires.

Please turn back to day 1 of this week, and review your list of moral standards that are acceptable today but fall short of God's standards. Can you think of anything else that would fail the Galatians 5 test? I have noted a couple of things to get you started:

- *Taking advantage of others in your workplace to make yourself look better to your boss* (selfish ambition, v. 20)
- *Being a party to division in your family or church* (discord, v. 20)
-
-
-

Reread Galatians 5:19–21 from the New Living Translation:

When you follow the desires of your sinful nature, your lives will produce these evil results: sexual immorality, impure thoughts, eagerness for lustful pleasure, idolatry, participation in demonic activities, hostility, quarreling, jealousy, outbursts of anger, selfish ambition, divisions, the feeling that everyone is wrong except those in your own little group, envy, drunkenness, wild parties, and other kinds of sin. Let me tell you again, as I have before, that anyone living that sort of life will not inherit the Kingdom of God.
—Galatians 5:19–21 (NLT)

Prayerfully ask God to use His Word to reveal areas of your life that fall below God's unchanging standard. Ask Him to be specific. Record what He reveals to you.

Read Romans 6:6–7. Compare it with Galatians 5:24–25. Summarize the truths found in these passages.

Now we are going to create a visual picture of a spiritual reality. God led me to do this one day during my time with Him. Don't skip ahead! Humor me, and you may be surprised at how much God can use a simple exercise to impact you with His truth.

   ✎ Inside the cross provided, write each specific sin that God brought to your mind earlier in this lesson. For example, this is one thing I wrote: "Selfishness—a desire for things to always be my way." As you write each item, confess it to your Lord. Agree with Him that it is sin, turn from it, and submit to obedience. Imagine that each sin is being nailed to the rough wood of the Cross of Christ. It is held in place by a large spike, driven in by a powerful hand. Continue as God directs. Use the margin if needed.

While I was writing this lesson, God brought to my mind the third verse of one of my favorite hymns. The Holy Spirit inspired Horatio G. Spafford to pen these words in 1873:

> *My sin—O the bliss of this glorious thought,*
> *My sin—not in part but the whole,*
> *Is nailed to the cross and I bear it no more,*
> *Praise the Lord, praise the Lord, O my soul!*
>   —Horatio G. Spafford, "It Is Well with My Soul"

Christ took *our* sins upon Himself on the Cross. He satisfied the penalty for our sins that justice demanded. Jesus took our sins and gave us His righteousness (2 Corinthians 5:21). Therefore, He calls us to live in freedom—

freedom to please God by living by the power of the Holy Spirit, not the freedom to satisfy our fleshly desires (Galatians 5:13). We cannot satisfy our sinful desires and fear God at the same time. Will you commit to a life of godly fear?

DAY 5

Obedience, the Follow-up to Repentance

Not long ago, I was driving in an area of Texas where I had never been. When it came time to change from one highway to another, I navigated the turn and headed off in a new direction. Thankfully I realized I was heading west instead of east before I had gone too far in the wrong direction. I had to exit the highway, go under it, turn around, and start driving the right way.

True repentance is just like that. When we are in sin, God calls to us to stop heading in the wrong direction. But stopping isn't enough. He also calls us to turn around and head in the right direction. He wants us to follow Him in obedience. In Malachi 3:6–10, God called Israel to stop, repent from their sin (robbing God), and then follow Him in obedience (bring the whole tithe). Jesus Christ (God the Son) calls for obedience—complete obedience—from those who follow Him.

Read Matthew 28:16–20.

Which of Jesus's teachings and commands does He want His followers to keep? Check all that apply:
- ❏ **Just the things that I would probably do anyway**
- ❏ **Those things that are not too difficult to obey**
- ❏ **Most of His commands, except those that require sacrifice or adjustment**
- ❏ **Absolutely everything that He commanded**

Use the definitions in the language notes on the far right to compose a statement that describes what Jesus expects, how many of His teachings and commands He wants His followers to keep, and what it means to keep them.

On day 3 of this week's study, we discussed the fact that God wants to bless the obedience of His children. Remember though, that the blessings God chooses to bring into our lives are not for our own benefit. God wants to use us as a channel to bless those around us. In Malachi, God promised the Israelites that He would bless their obedience in such a way that the world would sit up and take notice (Malachi 3:12). The fearful obedience of believers always points the world to God.

Read John 14:21–24. What does our obedience to God the Son reveal about us? What does our disobedience reveal?

In what ways are we blessed spiritually when we obey the words of Christ Jesus (vv. 21, 23)?

Read the following verse and answer this question: How can the lost world learn about God and our love for Him?

"But I will do what the Father requires of me, so that the world will know that I love the Father."

—John 14:31 (NLT)

How do we really feel about obeying God and His Word? My children have responded to my instruction with everything from the desire to please me to rebelling against the simplest instruction. Consistent obedience to God must stem from a proper heart attitude toward His instruction.

Read Psalm 119:57–64. Describe the attitude that the psalmist has about God's commands. (*Note:* Our Hebrew word for "fear," *yare'*, is found in verse 63.)

Language Notes

Matthew 28:20

English: **observe/keep**
Greek: *tereo*
Definition: attend to carefully; to take care of; to guard, to keep, to observe

English: **all**
Greek: *pas* (adjective)
Definition: each, every, any, all, or the whole

Yesterday we asked God to examine our lives and reveal specific areas of sin. Anytime God reveals our sin, it is for the purpose of repentance and obedience. I want to challenge you to follow through with repentance and return in every area of sin God revealed to you.

   Please review what you wrote on the cross in yesterday's lesson. In what specific ways can you follow your repentance with obedience? For example, if God revealed that you have been rude to a friend, you may need to go seek that friend's forgiveness.

   Will you commit to follow through on everything God told you to do? If so, write a prayer of commitment below.

WEEK 8

GOD MAKES FEARSOME DISTINCTION

It was Thanksgiving weekend. I was flying from my home in Calgary, Alberta, to visit my brother and his family in Idaho. As usual, I was running a little late for my flight. Check-in and security check went fairly quickly, so I was feeling good about making my plane until I rounded the last corner and entered the area for US Customs and Immigration. All six lines were backed up past the doorway. There was no way I would make my flight, having to wait in lines like those.

After standing in line for a few minutes, I had moved ahead just enough to notice this glorious little sign way off to the right. It read, "US citizens only," and a big, bold arrow pointed to a wonderfully short line. "US citizen—that's me!" I thought. While I happily hurried to the short line, I was careful not to gloat. I made it through customs in about five minutes, leaving behind several hundred frustrated Canadians. I made my flight and had a wonderful holiday.

I can imagine that every Canadian going through US Customs that morning felt that the special treatment given to US citizens was unfair. I even felt that way, though it did not stop me from waving my US passport. I guess the bottom line is this: The United States Department of Homeland Security has established guidelines for entering the United States. If you want to get in, you have to do it the prescribed way. If that department wants to distinguish between US citizens and noncitizens, it has the right.

This week of our study brings us to the climax of the Book of Malachi. We will see that God makes a distinction between persons who fear Him and those who do not. He has every right to do so. After all, He is God. The question is this: Which line will *we* be in?

DAY 1

Consumer Mentality

Before I had children, I worked in advertising. Although I left that field many years ago, I still have an interest in ad campaigns and slogans. You've probably heard the following:

"Because I'm worth it."

"Have it your way."

"I love what you do for me..."

Successful campaign slogans reveal a lot about the mentality of the American consumer. The statements above reflect the self-centeredness of our society. We have been taught that the world revolves around us individually. We tend to spend our money and time in ways that benefit us. Unfortunately, this consumer mentality has crept into the church. We shop for churches and serve God with the same attitudes we use to shop for a new car or enter a business deal: "Does this one meet my needs?" "What's in it for me?"

This attitude is nothing new. The people of Malachi's day wanted to know what they would get out of serving God. Hmmm... They, too, thought it was all about them.

As you will recall, Malachi begins with God's declaration of His love *for* Israel and His choosing *of* Israel. However, because of a lack of godly fear, the people chose their own sinful way. God confronted them with their rebellion. He warned them of the judgment to come and asked them to return to Him. God promised them blessings for their repentance and obedience. This is where we begin this week. How will the people respond to God's appeal to return?

In Malachi 3, we see two different responses to God's call to return. We will discuss both of these responses as we proceed through this week's study.

The first response we notice is the expression of harsh accusations against God. The people who responded this way complained that serving God was futile.

Read Malachi 3:13–18. Describe the attitude about God these people with the first response had, and discern how they felt about serving Him (v. 14).

Now read Malachi 3:14 from the New Living Translation:

"You have said, 'What's the use of serving God? What have we gained by obeying his commands or by trying to show the LORD Almighty that we are sorry for our sins?'"

—Malachi 3:14 (NLT)

Betsa' is the Hebrew word that is translated as "gain" or "profit" in Malachi 3:14. The *Theological Wordbook of the Old Testament* says the root word of *betsa'*, which is found in this verse, refers to "personal advantage derived from some activity."[1]

See the language notes below, and consider the definition of *betsa'* in Malachi 3:14. What do you think this "fearless" group of people expected to gain by serving God? Whose interests did they have in mind?

This same Hebrew word, *betsa'*, is used in Exodus 18. Moses was overwhelmed with settling disputes among the people of Israel. Therefore, his father-in-law, Jethro, advised him to appoint leaders to help with the task. Jethro even listed qualifications for these leaders.

Read Exodus 18:21. List these leadership qualifications below. (**Note:** The Hebrew words *yare'* [fear] and *betsa'* [gain/profit; helpfully rendered "bribe" in the English Standard Version] are both found in this verse.)

Do you think a connection exists between fearing God and not seeking personal gain? If so, what is it?

Language Notes

Malachi 3:14

English: **gain/profit**
Hebrew: *betsa'*
Definition: profit, unjust gain acquired by violence

When we fear God, our lives will be obediently yielded to His will and purposes. We will live to please God, not to fill our bank accounts or to find great success in business. Jesus also spoke about the desire for personal gain. He contrasted this worldly attitude with that of true discipleship.

Read Matthew 16:21–26. Why did Jesus rebuke Peter in verse 23?

Jesus had just told His followers that He was going to suffer and die at the hands of the Jewish leaders. This was certainly not what His disciples had in mind for their leader—or for themselves! But God's purpose was greater than a mere earthly kingdom. Jesus would establish a spiritual, eternal kingdom by conquering sin and death on the Cross. Once again, the desires of men conflicted with the will of God.

Reread Matthew 16:24–26. Now read the language notes below. Using the definition for *aparneomai*, the Greek word translated "deny," rewrite verse 24 in your own words.

List some things below that people seek to gain from this world.

What do you have to gain if you deny yourself and follow Christ?

The people described in Malachi 3:13–15 thought serving God was futile because they did not see any personal, worldly gain for them in it. They did not care about eternal matters or the will of God. It was all about what would benefit them in the here and now.

🕊 **In light of today's lesson, evaluate your service to God. What is your motivation?**

> **Language Notes**
>
> **Matthew 16:24–26**
>
> English: **deny**
> Greek: *aparneomai*
> Definition: to forget one's self, lose sight of one's own interests

☙ As we end today, meditate on the following words of Paul, and ask God to make them your own:

But whatever was to my profit I now consider loss for the sake of Christ. What is more, I consider everything a loss compared to the surpassing greatness of knowing Christ Jesus my Lord, for whose sake I have lost all things. I consider them rubbish, that I may gain Christ.

—Philippians 3:7–8

DAY 2

False Appearances

My friend Gina is the most gentle and caring person I know. She has a sweet smile and a soft, quiet voice. She is constantly encouraging others with cards, notes, and phone calls. She goes out of her way to help meet the needs of those around her. But if you ever have the occasion to play softball with Gina, don't let her peaceful spirit catch you off guard. On the field, she takes no prisoners! Gina plays first base on our coed, church softball team. She can reach farther than Stretch Armstrong to make the catch. Then she turns and genuinely apologizes to the runner who has just been called out at first.

One of the most amusing things to watch is Gina's first time at bat during a game. Because she is a woman, all the outfielders move in. Gina smiles and greets the catcher when she enters the batter's box. She may even give a little wave to the pitcher. The other team is thinking, "Automatic strike out." Then the pitch heads toward the plate. Gina positions her feet, hikes the bat, swings, and meets the ball. Then we all (all her teammates) shake our heads and laugh as the outfielders turn and run after the ball as it sails over their heads.

Things are not always as they seem. Appearances can be deceiving. I don't know how many times I have looked at circumstances and wondered if God was still in control. This doubt is as old as humanity. But our understanding is limited. We don't see what God sees. Our timing is not His. Today, we will consider the "fearless" Israelites' response to God about how things appeared. Then we will turn to God's Word for answers.

Read Malachi 3:14–15; then read language notes below. What do the people complain about in verse 15?

Has it ever seemed to you that those who faithfully serve God suffer, whereas the wicked prosper? Have you ever watched the ungodly continually succeed and accumulate wealth for their pleasure? We addressed some of these issues in week 6 when we studied Malachi 2:17 through 3:5. One truth we discovered is that God's judgment on evil is certain, but it will come in His timing. Another truth we discussed is that God does use life's circumstances to discipline and refine His children. Today we will revisit this topic of apparent injustice.

Read Psalm 73. What primary observation, found in verse 3, caused the psalmist to doubt God's goodness?

❧ Have you experienced similar doubts?

Describe the attitude and lifestyle of the arrogant and wicked as detailed in verses 4–12.

Summarize the psalmist's feelings of futility found in verses 13–16. Have you ever had similar feelings?

Language Notes

Malachi 3:15

English: **arrogant/proud**
Hebrew: *zed*
Definition: arrogant, proud, insolent, presumptuous

English: **workers of wickedness/ evildoers**
Hebrew: *`asah rish`ah*
Definition: to do, work, make, or produce wickedness

Reread pivotal verse 17. What experience helps the psalmist put his observations in the proper perspective? Summarize his new and correct attitude found in the last half of the psalm.

As humans, we naturally have a worldly, temporal perspective. Sin distorts the eternal truth of God. We must look at circumstances through the lens of His Word, from the position of being in His presence. The wicked will be destroyed. Although we don't know when, we are assured that their judgment is certain. But God holds His faithful ones with His right hand. He strengthens and guides them through this life. And when their time on earth is over, He takes them to eternal glory. Those whose hearts' desire is God need nothing else.

In the fourteenth century B.C., the young Egyptian Pharaoh Tutankhamen, commonly known today as King Tut, died after ruling for ten short years. The Egyptians, believing that great wealth would assure a resurrection, filled King Tut's tomb with priceless artifacts. Yet when British archaeologist Howard Carter discovered the tomb in 1922, King Tut's remains still laid in his solid-gold coffin surrounded by his wealth.[2] This finding provides convincing evidence that you really can't take it with you.

Read Psalm 49:5–10, 15–20. Describe how wealth can be deceptive. What is wealth unable to accomplish?

In whom does the psalmist put his trust for his eternal destination (v. 15)?

Some circumstances may not ever be different in this life, but eternity will reveal the truth. No amount of dependence on worldly wealth can save us.

Take time to reflect on your own life. Where have you put your trust? Do you depend on temporal things? If so, list them here, and ask God to redirect your trust and dependence to Him alone.

DAY 3

Roadblocks to Godly Fear

The Bible calls Satan a *"roaring lion"* that prowls around *"looking for someone to devour"* (1 Peter 5:8). Isn't it interesting that a group of lions is called a pride? It is our pride that so often allows us to fall prey to Satan's attacks. In Malachi 3:15, the arrogant or prideful are assumed to be *"blessed"* based on appearances. Yet the prideful are *"evildoers,"* and they *"challenge God."* Today, we are going to delve further into the issue of pride because this attitude of arrogance stifles godly fear.

> **Look up the definition for *pride*, and write it below. Don't stop at the first or second listing; make sure you include the negative dimensions of pride.**

You may have found that the first couple of listings for *pride* were fairly benign. The definition includes the ideas of self-esteem and self-respect. However, the full meaning of pride includes attitudes like arrogance, haughtiness, conceit, and an excessively high opinion of oneself.

> **Read 2 Corinthians 10:4–5 from the New Living Translation, as follows.**

> *We use God's mighty weapons, not mere worldly weapons, to knock down the Devil's strongholds. With these weapons we break down every proud argument that keeps people from knowing God. With these weapons we conquer their rebellious ideas, and we teach them to obey Christ.*
> —2 Corinthians 10:4–5 (NLT)

> **According to this 2 Corinthians passage, what is the sinful attitude that keeps people from knowing God?**

Pride is a human pretense that blocks us from knowing God. It is an unrealistic, inflated view of ourselves. When we do not view ourselves properly, we cannot have the proper perspective on God. Pride causes an inferior view of God and who He is. Not understanding, at least to some degree, the enormous greatness of God is the main reason for lack of godly fear. In *The Holiness of God*, R.C. Sproul addresses Isaiah's encounter with God, as recorded in Isaiah 6: "He saw the holiness of God. For the first time in his life, Isaiah really understood who God was. At the same instant, for the first time Isaiah really understood who Isaiah was."[3] It is only when we have a proper view of ourselves that we can even begin to have a proper view of God. Or is it the other way around? It is both!

> **Prayerfully consider your view of God. Is it big enough? Is it holy enough? If you think you have God figured out, then you have probably limited your view of who He is. The Scriptures tell us that God is beyond human comprehension. Write a prayer to God asking Him to remove any misconceptions you have about Him or yourself.**

Pride also has a way of creeping into our ideas about salvation. In our minds, we know that our works cannot save us. Even the best of our works are like filthy rags compared to the holiness of God. Yet we often puff up with spiritual pride when we compare our lives with someone else's. Paul wrote to the Christians in Philippi about this issue:

> *For we who worship God in the Spirit are the only ones who are truly circumcised. We put no confidence in human effort. Instead, we boast about what Christ Jesus has done for us. Yet I could have confidence in myself if anyone could. If others have reason for confidence in their own efforts, I have even more! For I was circumcised when I was eight days old, having been born into a pure-blooded Jewish family that is a branch of the tribe of Benjamin. So I am a real Jew if there ever was one! What's more, I was a member of the Pharisees, who demand the strictest obedience to the Jewish law. And zealous? Yes, in fact, I harshly persecuted the church. And I obeyed the Jewish law so carefully that I was never accused of any fault.*
> —Philippians 3:3–6 (NLT)

In the passage on the previous page, circle all the reasons that Paul could have had for spiritual pride. Think of contemporary reasons that are similar to those of Paul's, and list them below.

✦ Have you ever been guilty of allowing these or similar reasons to become a source of pride?

Spiritual pride is the false notion that we have, even in a small way, had something to do with our own salvation. This sin is as old as Christianity itself. In Paul's letter to the church in Rome, he warns them to be on their guard against spiritual pride. In this warning, Paul used Abraham, the great patriarch, as an example:

> Abraham was, humanly speaking, the founder of our Jewish nation. What were his experiences concerning this question of being saved by faith? Was it because of his good deeds that God accepted him? If so, he would have had something to boast about. But from God's point of view Abraham had no basis at all for pride. For the Scriptures tell us, "Abraham believed God, so God declared him to be righteous." When people work, their wages are not a gift. Workers earn what they receive. But people are declared righteous because of their faith, not because of their work.
>
> —Romans 4:1–5 (NLT)

According to this passage from Romans, in what might Abraham have taken pride? Why was Abraham declared righteous by God?

On what basis does God declare us righteous?

What part do our good deeds play?

God makes it clear that pride is sin. It is also an attitude that fosters other sin. *"God opposes the proud,"* but He lifts up the humble (1 Peter 5:5). Humility is the proper attitude we should have before our holy God. Pride causes us to have a *higher* view of ourselves than we should; humility fosters a *proper* view of ourselves. Yet humility does not negate the working of God in and through our lives.

Read Romans 12:3–8. Based on this passage, write a definition for godly humility.

How is this proper view of self manifested in the life of a believer?

Humility does not negate our self-worth. God chose us in love to be His own. He filled us with His Spirit and gave us gifts to use in His service. If we think lower of ourselves than we should, we are denying the grace of God in our lives.

 Have you ever been guilty of false humility? Have you ever refused to allow God to use your life in a specific way because you felt "humbly" inadequate? Record anything God brings to your mind.

Believers, we must ask God to give us a proper view of ourselves. A proper view is based completely on who God is. When we recognize the great holiness of God, there will be no basis for pride in our lives. Our response will be godly fear and a humble spirit that produces a radical obedience and availability to the manifest power of God.

> *True humility and fear of the* LORD *lead to riches, honor, and long life.*
> —Proverbs 22:4 (NLT)

DAY 4

The Drawing of the Line

The Bible records that many Gentiles became proselytes of the Jewish faith. They were often referred to as *God-fearers*. Rabbinical law distinguished between *half* proselytes and *full* proselytes: Half proselytes were asked to conform to only a limited portion of the law, but as a result, they were allowed only limited participation in the synagogue. Full, or devout, proselytes were bound to all the Mosaic ceremonial law, including circumcision. This commitment granted them full participation and fellowship in the local synagogue.[4]

Nehemiah 10:28 describes just such a group of converted Gentiles as those *"who separated themselves from the neighboring peoples for the sake of the Law of God."* In order to follow the one, true God, these full-fledged God-fearers left their old way of life and committed themselves to Him spiritually, emotionally, intellectually, and physically. They crossed the line. They were no longer pagans or even *half* God-fearers; they were *full* God-fearers.

Malachi 3 records a similar distinction that God makes between two groups of people. Those who choose to fear God and those God refers to as wicked or "evildoers." These wicked people are the ones God was talking to in Malachi 3:5. In that verse, the Lord God said they did not fear Him.

In Hebrew, when *not* is used with a verb, like *fear*, it means "absolute prohibition." Therefore, the wicked evildoers in Malachi—the ones whom God would judge—had absolutely no fear of God. This concept is significant. Where there is no fear of God, there is no fear of judgment. Where there is no fear of judgment, there is no repentance. Those who have absolutely no fear of God will not repent of their sin to accept God's forgiveness. Everyone who receives God's salvation has at least some measure of godly fear. Yet Christians who fear God a little are like half God-fearers. They cannot experience the full measure of all that a deep relationship with God has to offer. Therefore, it should be our goal as Christians to be full-fledged God-fearers, ones who are in a position to abundantly experience all of God's blessings.

Read Malachi 3:14–18. Summarize the differences in attitude toward God between persons who feared Him and those who did not.

Reread verse 18. What word and phrase does God use to describe the God-fearers?

What word and phrase does God use to describe those who have no fear of Him?

God has identified two distinct groups of people. It is as if He has drawn a line in the sand and said, "Everyone who fears Me and chooses to serve Me, stand on this side; and everyone who has no fear of Me and will not serve Me, stand on that side." God does not give us the option of straddling the line. If you are going to serve God, you must step across. If you are a Christian—if you have repented of your sins and given your life to Jesus—you have crossed the line from being the wicked to being a God-fearer. But does your life reveal a Christian who is a half God-fearer or a full God-fearer?

Recently, I took my oldest daughter to freshman orientation at the University of North Texas. There was a Mean Green Eagle spirit dinner the last night of orientation. During the program, they called one particular student-to-be up to the podium. This young man was wearing a burnt orange, University of Texas Longhorn hat. The master of ceremonies was kind but firm when he insisted the student trade in his Longhorn cap for a green UNT cap. Although the episode was lighthearted and humorous, the line had been drawn. The University of North Texas does not want divided loyalties.

But how often do we try to do the same thing with God? We may give Him our 10 percent, but we try to maintain control of the other 90 percent. We are obedient in most areas of our lives, but in spots, sin still has free reign. Jesus said we can't serve two masters. We will hate one and love the other (Matthew 6:24). We can't straddle the line; we must make a choice.

Near the end of the Book of Joshua, we are told that the Lord had driven out Israel's enemies from the Promised Land and given His people rest (Joshua 23:1, 9). Joshua, their leader, knowing he was close to death, summoned the people to Shechem. After reminding them of all that God had done, he set a choice before them.

Read Joshua 24:14–24. What is the choice that Joshua asked the Israelites to make?

Could they choose to serve the Lord along with some of the pagan gods?

Reread verse 14 from the New American Standard Bible, as follows:

"Now, therefore, fear the LORD *and serve Him in sincerity and truth; and put away the gods which your fathers served beyond the River and in Egypt, and serve the* LORD*."*

—Joshua 24:14 (NASB)

If the Israelites chose to serve God, to what were they committing? Use the language notes below to help you with your answer.

Joshua did not leave any room for divided allegiance. After the people made an initial commitment in verse 18 to serve God, Joshua issued a warning. He told them that serving God would not be as easy as they thought. God is jealous and demands complete loyalty. But the people insisted they wanted to serve God.

Reread verses 23–24. What direction did Joshua give the people to prepare their lives for total commitment to God?

🐦 **Examine your own life. Are any "foreign gods" interfering with your ability to completely yield your heart and life to God?**

> ### Language Notes
> #### Joshua 24:14
>
> English: **fear/revere**
> Hebrew: *yare'*
> Definition: to fear, revere, be afraid
>
> English: **faithfulness/sincerity**
> Hebrew: *tamiym*
> Definition: complete, whole, entire, sound
>
> English: **truth**
> Hebrew: *'emeth*
> Definition: firmness, faithfulness, truth, sureness, reliability

If so, will you throw them out now? Yes No I need God's help. (Circle one.)

Throughout our study of Malachi, we have heard God plead His case before His people. He chose them in love to be His, but in rebellion they went their own way. God reminded them of His justice and warned them of His judgment. He called them to return. Even then, many continued on a path of destruction. But a few chose to fear the Lord. When God drew the line in the sand, they stepped across to His side.

🕊 **On which side of the line will you take your stand?**

🕊 **As we end today, please reflect on the words of Joshua.**

"Choose for yourselves this day whom you will serve.... But as for me and my household, we will serve the LORD."

—Joshua 24:15

Day 5

God's Remembrance of Those Who Fear Him

I make scrapbooks in my spare time. I began doing this in high school, long before scrapbooking became a hot, or popularized, activity. In addition to general family books, I create books for special occasions or beloved people. For instance, as my husband's 40th birthday approached, I spent several months putting together a book to commemorate that milestone. I asked Wayne's mom to send baby pictures, and I contacted his friends from childhood and early adult years to send photos and greetings. The gift was a hit.

The scrapbooks I've created are among my family's most treasured possessions because they are much more than paper and ink. They tell stories and store memories. They symbolize love and relationships. They are a record of God's blessings in our lives.

The God-fearers in the Book of Malachi made a special book or scroll to record how they felt about God. God watched with pleasure. Today we will study the wonderful truth that God recognizes and remembers those who fear Him.

Read Malachi 3:16–18. List the ways found in these verses that God gives special recognition or blessing to those who fear Him.

You may have written that God *"listened and heard"* them at the top of your list. Just imagine. The God who holds the universe together listens to those who fear Him. Malachi 3:16 states that *"those who feared the LORD talked with each other, and the LORD listened and heard."* What do you think they were saying? Malachi does not give us that information, but I have an idea. I believe those faithful few joined together to strengthen and encourage each other in their commitment to the Lord. They may have realized that God created His people for community, and that it is harder to stay true to God if you try to stand alone among the "fearless."

The God-fearers, those persons who committed to honor God with their lives and serve Him wholeheartedly, formed a kind of accountability group. I believe they made a commitment to help each other remain faithful to God. They recorded this momentous occasion on a scroll as God looked on with approval. God's response to the commitment of the God-fearers was incredible! God claimed them as His *"treasured possession"* (v. 17) and made a promise to spare them when He comes in judgment.

The Hebrew word *cgullah*, translated as "treasured possession" in the New International Version, is found only eight times in the Old Testament. Twice it refers to a king's collection of silver and gold. Five times God uses the term in reference to Israel, the nation He chose and set apart for Himself. The eighth time is here in Malachi. See language notes below.

Read Exodus 19:3–8. (*Note:* The appearance of *cgullah* in verse 5 is the first occurrence of that word in the Scriptures.)

Although God claimed Israel as His special treasure, He attached conditions to this very unique relationship. What were they (v. 5)?

Language Notes

Malachi 3:17

English: **treasured possession**
Hebrew: *cgullah*
Definition: possession, property, valued property, peculiar treasure

---

What was the purpose (v. 6), of this special relationship between God and the nation of Israel?

The only time the Hebrew word for "treasured possession" is used to refer to a group of people other than the nation of Israel as a whole is here in Malachi 3:17.

Why do you think God now uses this term for the God-fearing remnant of Israel instead of the nation as a whole?

Again, God-fearers are persons who have committed to honor God with their lives and serve Him wholeheartedly. They also serve as priests of the New Covenant, sharing Christ with a lost world. God hears them and listens intently. He will remember them when the day of His judgment comes; with fatherly love, He will spare them. Scripture is full of promises that God makes to those who fear Him. Let's look at a few from the Book of Psalms.

Read each of the following passages and record God's promise to those who fear Him. (**Note:** Each of these passages includes a form of *yare'*, the Hebrew word for "fear," which we have noted throughout this study. Depending on your translation, *yare'* may appear as "reverence," "awe," or some other variant.)

- **Psalm 25:14**

- **Psalm 31:19**

- **Psalm 33:18–19**

- **Psalm 103:13**

- **Psalm 115:11**

- **Psalm 145:19**

These verses and others emphasize the truth that God recognizes and blesses those who fear Him. For the last eight weeks, we have sought to define this biblical attitude through studying the Book of Malachi. God confronts His rebellious people with their sin, attributing their waywardness to a lack of godly fear. We have used the lives of these fearless ones as a case study to teach us what it means *to fear* God. We have one week of study remaining. We will examine the remaining chapter of Malachi, review what we have learned over the course of the study, and consider ways to foster godly fear in our lives.

Before we end today, please consider this very important question: Will you make a commitment to fear God and honor His name like the people described in Malachi 3:16 did? If so, write a statement below declaring your commitment to God. Sign it and date it in His presence. This is your "scroll of remembrance." Based on your commitment, you can then write your name in the blanks below.

"_____ will be mine," says the Lord *Almighty, "in the day when I make up my treasured possession. I will spare _____ , just as in compassion a man spares his son who serves him."*

—Malachi 3:17 (personalized)

WEEK 9

GOD DELIGHTS IN THOSE
WHO FEAR HIM

Today we begin our last week together. God taught me so much while I was writing this study. I pray for you that the past eight weeks have been a time of spiritual growth and deepened commitment to the God we both serve.

I know we have covered a lot of ground. This week will bring it all together. On days 1 and 2, we will see that our decision to fear or not to fear God definitely brings eternal results. On days 3 and 4, we will review the past eight weeks, identifying important aspects of godly fear. On day 5, we will study the last three verses, or epilogue, of Malachi, using them as a springboard to discover how we can foster godly fear in our lives.

The purpose of this study is threefold: first, to show through Scriptures that fearing God is a positive attitude that God commands His children to have; second, to better understand the meaning of godly fear by studying the original language and considering biblical descriptions; and third, to encourage you to commit to a life of godly fear. If we want to live a life pleasing to God, the Scriptures teach that we must fear Him.

His pleasure is not in the strength of the horse, nor his delight in the legs of a man; the LORD delights in those who fear him, who put their hope in his unfailing love.

—Psalm 147:10–11

DAY 1

God's Judgment Fire

My family and I moved to Casper, Wyoming, during the dry summer of 1988. Although Casper was a five-hour drive from Yellowstone

National Park, we could see and smell the smoke from the record-setting forest fires that ravaged the area that year. By the middle of July, the fire activity was out of control. When the last of the fires was finally put out in November, over a third of the park (nearly 800,000 acres) had burned.[1]

When we visited Yellowstone early the next summer, we noticed the stark contrast between the areas that had burned and those that had not. Lush, green forest met blackened, barren wasteland where nothing remained but a few charred tree trunks.

Although not a perfect analogy, I thought of these fires as I read Malachi 4.

Read Malachi 4:1–3 from the New Living Translation:

The LORD Almighty says, "The day of judgment is coming, burning like a furnace. The arrogant and the wicked will be burned up like straw on that day. They will be consumed like a tree—roots and all. But for you who fear my name, the Sun of Righteousness will rise with healing in his wings. And you will go free, leaping with joy like calves let out to pasture. On the day when I act, you will tread upon the wicked as if they were dust under your feet," says the LORD Almighty.

—Malachi 4:1–3 (NLT)

This passage immediately follows Malachi 3:16–18, the passage that reveals God will make a distinction between those who fear Him and those who do not. Again, in the first three verses of Malachi 4, God clearly states that those who fear His name will be treated differently on His day of judgment than those who do not fear His name. Recall our discussion about the use of the word *not* with a verb like *fear* in Hebrew: it means absolute prohibition. While Christians have varying degrees of godly fear, the wicked—those who will suffer in the fires of God's judgment—have absolutely no fear of God.

Write the facts you find in Malachi 4:1–3 concerning what will happen on Judgment Day to those who have no fear of God (the wicked and arrogant).

Read 2 Thessalonians 1:5–10. How does Paul describe those who will receive God's punishment (v. 8)?

Does this description remind you of anything we've been learning about people who have absolutely no fear of God? Individuals destined for eternal destruction don't even fear God enough to realize they are sinners and recognize their need for a Savior!

According to 2 Thessalonians 1:7, how will Jesus be revealed when He comes with judgment from heaven? How is this picture similar to God's judgment as described in Malachi 4:1–3?

Throughout the Scriptures, heat, fire, and light are used as metaphors for the nature and ways of God. As we will see in Malachi 4, sometimes the metaphor is used positively and sometimes negatively. The source, God, is constant, never changing; the results vary, depending on how and to whom the heat, fire, or light is applied.

Although siblings, my brother and I react very differently to the sun. I tan very easily. Even if I get a little sunburned, by the next day, the pink turns brown. My brother, however, burns easily, sometimes severely. Once on a family vacation to Florida, my parents had to take him to a local emergency room to be treated for blistering and sun poisoning.

God's application of judgment will reveal a distinction between the wicked and the righteous. In Malachi 3:2–4, God's fire is described as a refining fire that will purify His people. In Malachi 4:1, His fire is depicted as one of punishment and destruction. But why will the "fire" of the one God affect different people differently?

Read 1 Corinthians 3:10–15. Based on this passage, describe why God's same judgment fire will affect individual lives differently.

The Book of Hebrews tells us that God is a *"consuming fire"* and will destroy all temporal things, including persons who are disobedient and rebellious toward God. But the eternal—those things that cannot be shaken—will remain. This fact should cause us to worship Him with godly fear (Hebrews 12:25–29). The passage we read from 1 Corinthians 3 teaches that on Judgment Day, even the quality of the lives of believers will be tested by God's fire. Believers will be saved, but their works may be consumed by God's judgment.

꩜ **Please pause before ending your study time today, and take a personal inventory. Have you built your life on the eternal foundation of Jesus Christ? If so, what kind of materials are you using to build on that foundation? Are you investing your time and energy in things that have lasting value? What are these things?**

DAY 2

God's Saving Light

W ho imagined the sun and gives source to its light…." Christian music artist Chris Tomlin heightens our awe of God as he praises our Creator through the words of the song "Indescribable," written by Laura Story. I am awestruck when I consider all of God's careful planning in creation and His provision for human life through the placement of the sun. The sun is much more than just the center of our solar system. Without the sun, life on planet earth would not be possible. Our atmosphere gets its power for wind and rain from the sun. The oxygen in the air we breathe is generated when plants use the sun's rays to make their food. The sun dictates day and night, seasons, and time.

Although the light and heat from the sun are both beneficial and necessary for life, too much exposure without protection can be dangerous. Our skin may develop cancer and will show increased signs of aging if we fail to protect it with sunscreen. Prolonged viewing of the sun with the naked eye can cause yellowing of the lens and cornea and can increase the chance of cataracts. Viewing the sun through devices that concentrate the light, such as binoculars, without using a special filter can cause permanent blindness.

In our day 1 study this week, we saw in Malachi 4:1 that God likened His judgment to a blast furnace. His consuming fire will one day judge those who are arrogant and evil, those who have no fear of His name. Yet in the very next verse, God describes Himself and the day of His coming differently. Note the metaphor He uses to describe Himself.

Read Malachi 4:1–3. How does God describe Himself in verse 2?

In the ancient Near East, the winged disk of the sun was used to represent a source of protection and blessing.[2] Malachi and the people of his day would have been very familiar with this idea. But for the people of God, it is more than a concept—it is a reality. God is the true and ultimate source of protection and blessing.

What characteristic distinguishes the group of people that God will protect and bless from the group that God will judge with fire (v. 2)?

God's name is synonymous with His character, the essence of who He is. When we fear His name, we fear Him. A person who fears God is one who responds to Him and His holy nature correctly. Under the New Covenant, a person who has responded appropriately has, first of all, realized that the only way he or she can approach God is through Christ and His sacrifice. Over the next two days, as we review the study, we will compile more characteristics of one who fears God. But for the purpose of today's lesson, we need to realize that the first characteristic of a New Testament God-fearer is that he or she has been saved through the blood of Jesus. Eternally secure in Christ, a believer is free to experience the healing power of *"the Sun of Righteousness"* (Malachi 4:2 NLT).

Read the passages in table 9 that describe the *"light of the world,"* and complete the table.

Table 9. Jesus Christ, the Light of the world

SCRIPTURE	WORD OR PHRASE USED TO DESCRIBE CHRIST	HEALING RESULTS OF THE LIGHT OF CHRIST
Isaiah 9:2, 6–7 (**Note:** Verse 2 is quoted in Matthew 4:14–16.)		

Table 1 is continued on next page.

Scripture	Word or phrase used to describe Christ	Healing results of the light of Christ
Luke 1:76–79 (*Note:* This is part of Zechariah's prophecy concerning his son, John the Baptist.)		
John 1:4–5, 9		
John 8:12		

🕊 **Prayerfully consider how you have personally experienced the healing power of "*the Sun of Righteousness.*" Write a prayer of thanksgiving to God.**

God does not want us to miss the important fact that He will make a distinction between persons who fear Him and those who do not fear Him. In the middle of Malachi 4:2, God uses a new metaphor to make sure we get it. I have never witnessed a calf being released from a stall, but I have been present several times when our black Lab was released from her traveling kennel after a long car ride. She would wear herself out, running frantic, joyful circles around the yard. Those who have been bound appreciate freedom the most.

For those who fear God, Judgment Day will be a time of rejoicing. Nothing will remain of wickedness except the ashes under our feet as we dance in celebration (Malachi 4:3). Jesus's victory over sin and death, which He accomplished on the Cross, will be fulfilled. Sometimes Christians today, myself included, become discouraged when we see the *apparent* victory of evil in the world. Just like the people Malachi described, we ask God why He does not do something. Yet we need only remember His promises. Malachi 4:1–3 is one picture of God's complete triumph over evil.

Read Romans 16:20. How does this verse compare with the picture portrayed in Malachi 4:3?

As a believer, what promise of God can you claim for your own life?

Believer, God *is* and *will be* completely victorious. If you belong to Christ, your eternal future is secure. Why not do a little joyful leaping before your Lord today?

DAY 3

Review: Part 1

As I looked back at what we have studied the last eight weeks, I must admit, I was overwhelmed. God has shown us many things through the Book of Malachi. However, for the sake of time, I must condense our review to only a few highlights. I encourage you to review what we have covered more thoroughly as you have time.

The purpose of our study these next two days is to help us grasp what it means to fear God. As we work through these two sessions, I will ask you several times to add certain information to the "Picture of fear" table (table 10) at the end of this week's day 4 study (p. 158). We will be filling this table with characteristics of persons who fear God and of those who do not. By the end of day 4, this character study will provide us with an awesome word picture of biblical, godly fear. Let's get started.

Week 1: God Deserves Our Fear

We began our study together by establishing that the fear of God is a positive biblical principle. We read a selection of passages from throughout the Bible that revealed a contrast between those who fear God and those who do not.

Review table 1 from week 1, day 1. Record significant characteristics from that table on the Picture of fear table (table 10) at the end of this week's day 4 study. Keep in mind that for the purposes

of this table, we are looking for attitudes and characteristics associated with fearing God and not fearing God; we are not recording results, such as God's discipline or blessings.

We learned from the Scriptures that God not only deserves our fear, but He demands it. Therefore, God seeks to foster fear of Himself in the lives of His children. We looked to the nation of Israel for an example.

Read Deuteronomy 4:9–14. What did the nation of Israel experience at the foot of Mount Horeb (Mount Sinai)? What was God's purpose for this encounter?

Don't miss this! God allowed His people to experience His holiness so they would *fear* Him. God wanted them to fear Him to produce lives of *obedience*. (You can add this to your table 10.) But there is something else that godly fear will produce.

"Who will not fear, O Lord, and glorify Your name? For You alone are holy; for ALL THE NATIONS WILL COME AND WORSHIP BEFORE YOU, FOR YOUR RIGHTEOUS ACTS HAVE BEEN REVEALED."

—Revelation 15:4 (NASB)

As a reminder, what should cause us to fear God? Besides obedience, what else should godly fear produce in our lives? Add these things to table 10.

Week 2: God Declares His Love

One way that God expresses His holy nature is through His love. In week 2, we saw that Malachi begins with God's declaration of love for His people. We reviewed that love through Israel's history. Believer, just like God chose the children of Israel because He loved them, God chose you because He loves you!

Read Ephesians 1:3–5. What kind of life does God want for His chosen ones?

Week 3: God Describes a "Fearless" Life

In Malachi's day, God's people were not living the kind of life He wanted for His chosen ones. Why? God pinned it on a lack of godly fear. One of the first symptoms we discovered in Malachi of this deficit was the offering of defiled sacrifices to God (Malachi 1:6–14).

> **Read Romans 12:1–2. What *"sacrifice"* does God require from us as New Covenant believers? In what condition does He expect our sacrifice to be?**

Defiled lives dishonor God's name (Malachi 1:12). Those who do not fear Him will live defiled lives by conforming to the world and its ways. Holy lives bring His name honor. Those who fear God will obediently seek to live holy lives.

> **Read Deuteronomy 10:12–13 for a description of a life that fears God. Add the characteristics you find in this passage to table 10.**

Week 4: God's Covenant Demands Fear

In week 4, we studied about God's covenant with the original Levites. God desired to bring the nation life and peace through His covenant with them. The success of this covenant required that the Levites fear God. However, Malachi's generation of Levites did not fear God.

> **Read Malachi 2:5–9. Review table 5, from the week 4, day 2 session. Add the "fearful" and "fearless" characteristics noted there to your table 10.**

Like the Levitical priests of the Old Covenant, we are priests of the New Covenant in Christ. But this is not a covenant written on tablets of stone; rather, it is a covenant written on the hearts of believers (Hebrews 8:10). Some would say that persons under the New Covenant do not need to fear God. But what did Jesus say?

Read Matthew 10:28–33. For those who trust in God, what is there no need to fear? What should we fear? Add discoveries from this passage to your Picture of fear table (table 10).

Before we end today, we should review one more key concept that we covered in the first half of our study, beginning in week 3, day 1: the proper tension that should exist in our relationship with God. Malachi 1:6 declares that God is our *Father* and our *Master*. We are both *child* and *slave*. Leaning too much in either direction will bring an imbalance in our relationship. If we consider God only as our Father, then we may become too casual with God. We are in danger of not taking our sin seriously and taking advantage of His mercy and grace. Yet if we see God merely as our Master, then we will miss out on the glorious blessings that come from an intimate relationship with our loving, heavenly Father. When we live in the balance between the two, we live a life of godly fear.

Add characteristics to table 10 based on the previous paragraph.

Prayerfully ask God to reveal to you if an imbalance in your relationship with Him exists. Ask Him to show you the adjustments you need to make.

DAY 4

Review: Part 2

I pray that yesterday's review helped you begin to formulate a clear picture of biblical, godly fear. We will continue our review today. We have four more weeks to cover, so there's no time to waste.

Week 5: God Denounces Worldly Compromise

In week 5, we learned that worldly compromise is nothing less than disobedience. The marrying of pagan wives is the example of compromise in Malachi 2:10–16. In Deuteronomy 7:1–6, God had commanded Israel to completely rid the land of the pagan ways around them. Why? Because any compromise with the ways of the world, no matter how small, had the potential for spiritual disaster. When the Jewish men married pagan wives, it led them to idolatry.

Add "worldly compromise" and "complete obedience" in the appropriate columns in your "Picture of fear" table (table 10) at the end of today's study.

Turn to week 5, day 3, and review what God revealed to you about areas of compromise in your own life. Have you made any progress in these areas in the last four weeks?

We identified a cure for compromise from the Scriptures. Using God's commands from Malachi 2:15–16 regarding this specific situation and the record of a similar occurrence in Ezra 10, we established four components of dealing with the sin of compromise.

Please turn to week 5, day 5, and review these four components. Write them here.

**Read Malachi 2:16. Focus on the latter part of the verse.
Add to table 10 additional insight regarding protecting yourself from compromise.**

When we live before God with an attitude of fear, the four components of dealing with the sin of compromise just reviewed will be a constant, ongoing part of our lives. In addition to actively guarding ourselves from compromise, we will regularly, as part of our time with God, ask Him to reveal areas of sin. We will then respond with repentance and do whatever it takes to remove sin from our lives. Then we will seek restoration with God and any others whom our compromises have affected.

Add to table 10 the characteristics that came to light during this session's discussion on worldly compromise.

Week 6: God Demonstrates His Justice

In week 6, we explored how God's justice is expressed in the lives of both believers and unbelievers. The people of Malachi's day questioned God's justice because they saw the wicked prosper (Malachi 2:17). God assured them of His judgment of the wicked (Malachi 3:5). Believers, because

Christ has already received the punishment for our sins, we do not have to fear the judgment. However, the realization that God *does* judge should foster godly fear in us, as believers. This fear will then find expression in our lives.

> **Read 2 Peter 3:9–14. What should believers do with the knowledge that God does not want anyone to perish?**

> **In light of the reality of God's judgment, what kind of lives should believers live?**

> **Add the characteristics above to the appropriate columns in your table 10.**

Although believers do not have to fear God's eternal condemnation, God's justice still works in our lives. God's purpose is for His children to be holy. In days 2 through 5 of week 6, we considered three appropriate means of justice that God uses in our lives to keep us progressing toward holiness: disciplining, refining or purifying, and sharing in the sufferings of Christ. (Please review week 6 if you need a reminder about the distinction between these.)

> **Read the following passages. Identify God's method of justice in each passage, and note what kind of attitude a "fearful" believer should have toward God in the process.**
> - **Hebrews 12:7–11**
> - **1 Peter 1:6–8**
> - **1 Peter 4:12–19**

> **Please add this information to your table 10.**

Week 7: God Deplores "Fearless" Detours

The topic of week 7 was spiritual detours. In Malachi, God called His people to return to Him from their detour. They asked God in what way they had strayed. One example God gave them was robbery or withholding their tithes. Tithing requires that we give God our first and our best. In Deuteronomy 14:22–23, God says that the purpose of the tithe is for His people to learn to fear Him. As New Covenant believers, although we are not bound to the letter of the law, we should desire to follow the spirit of the law. In 2 Corinthians 9:6–15, we discovered principles for giving that should take us beyond a mere 10 percent of our financial resources.

> **How do you think giving God our first and best of everything can teach us to fear Him? Read 1 Timothy 6:17–19 to help with your answer.**

Remember that robbing God is merely one example of how believers can take a spiritual detour. Any time we go our own way, we stray from God's path. What is considered acceptable or not acceptable in our society changes with every generation; however, God's way never changes because His nature is constant and unchangeable (Malachi 3:6).

> **Read Malachi 3:6–7. Have you allowed yourself to be swayed by cultural norms?   Yes   No   (Circle one.)**

> **If yes, God calls you to repent and return to Him. Record anything God reveals to you.**

Fearful believers recognize that God's ways and His expectations for His children are unchanging. Fearful believers do not regularly follow the world. But when they do fall and detour from God's path, fearful believers repent and return.

> **Make additions to your table 10 regarding giving and the unchanging nature of God.**

Week 8: God Makes Fearsome Distinction

Last week, we emphasized that God makes a distinction between those who fear Him and those who do not fear Him. Malachi 3:13–18 compares these two groups' responses to God's call to repent and return. Remember, the fearless group served God for what they could get out of it (Malachi 3:14), and the fearful group served God to bring honor to His name (Malachi 3:16).

Read Malachi 3:14–16 again, and notice the attitudes of these two groups. Identify characteristics in this passage that you can add to your table 10.

We don't have enough time or space to review in detail all the wonderful truths we gleaned in this second half of our study together. However, a few things were noted that you will want to add to your Picture of fear table. We found that pride is a deterrent to godly fear, but God will lift up the humble (Malachi 3:18 through 4:1 and 1 Peter 5:5–6). We learned that serving God with an attitude of fear means we cannot straddle the fence; it requires total commitment and undivided allegiance (Malachi 3:18 and Joshua 24:14–24).

Please add any helpful information from previous paragraph to your table 10.

As we ended week 8, we saw in the Scriptures that God not only recognizes but also blesses those who fear Him. Do you desire to commit to live your life serving God with a proper attitude of fear? If so, review your Picture of fear table and ask God to help you truly understand what godly fear looks like.

Table 10. Picture of fear

FEARLESS CHARACTERISTICS	FEARFUL CHARACTERISTICS

After reviewing your Picture of fear table, summarize here what you believe it means to fear God.

As we close today, write a prayer of commitment to God, expressing your desire to live a life of godly fear.

DAY 5

The Fostering of Godly Fear

How often do you look in the mirror to make sure your physical appearance is acceptable? I usually check things out several times a day. I have to make sure there isn't any food between my teeth or mustard on my mouth. I want to know if a lock of hair has decided to do something interesting. If I find something that needs correcting or cleaning—and I often do—then I correct it or clean it before anyone else sees me.

Over these last nine weeks, we have looked into the mirror of God's Word. You must now decide what to do with what you have seen. Will you merely accept it as more head knowledge and walk away? Or will you commit to applying the truth of God's Word to your life? If you choose the latter, then today's lesson is for you. This last day together, we will explore how to foster godly fear in our own lives.

Please read Malachi 4:4–6.

These last three verses of the Book of Malachi are an epilogue. It is the *what now* for everything that has come before. God had spoken to His people through the prophet Malachi. Beginning from a position of love, He confronted them with their disobedience. They had sinned and brought dishonor to God's name because they did not fear Him as they should have. He assured them that judgment would be coming. He called them to repent and return to Him.

The people responded in two different ways: One group, the "fearless," refused to repent and leave their sin. But another group, those who feared the Lord, the "fearful," responded positively to His call and honored His name. God made it clear that on Judgment Day, He will make a distinction between those who fear Him and those who do not. The fearful will be God's treasured possession. The fearless will be eternally judged for their disobedience. In the epilogue, God detailed how He wanted them to live in light of this truth.

Remember God's Word

First, God told the people to remember the Law of Moses, which was given on Mount Horeb (Malachi 4:4). This directive pointed the people back to God's Word and His covenant with them. The Hebrew word *zakar,* translated as "remember" in the NIV, implies much more than not forgetting; see language notes below. *Remembering,* according to the *Theological Wordbook of the Old Testament,* results in actions, such as meditating on, paying attention to, proclaiming, and confessing. It reminds me of James 1:22. Hearing or remembering God's Word is not enough. We must do what it says. God wants His people to *remember His Word* because it helps foster godly fear in their lives.

> **Read Deuteronomy 17:18–20. Although this passage was specifically directed to the man God would choose to be king of His people, the principle definitely applies to us. According to this passage, how can we foster godly fear?** (*Note: Yare'* is found in verse 19. Depending on your translation, it may be rendered "fear" or "revere" in English.)

Fostering godly fear in our lives requires more than just a cursory reading of God's Word. It takes diligence and a commitment to read and study it regularly.

Read Proverbs 2:1–5. Describe the kind of attention and response to God's Word that is required to "understand the fear of the LORD" (v. 5).

Language Notes
Malachi 4:4
English: **remember**
Hebrew: *zakar*
Definition: to remember, recall, call to mind

Heed the Message of Elijah

In Malachi's epilogue, God declared He would send the prophet Elijah before coming in judgment. In the Scriptures, the name *Elijah* can represent other prophets who come in a role like Elijah's. We have already seen in this study that John the Baptist is one example. John's message was one of repentance and preparation for the Lord's coming. Therefore, between now and the second coming of Christ for judgment, God will be calling His people to repentance and preparation.

> **Read Psalm 130:1–4. How do you think coming to God in repentance can foster godly fear?**

Repentance accompanied by receiving God's forgiveness is the first step in preparing for God's Judgment Day. Yes, persons whose sins are covered by the blood of Christ will receive eternal salvation. But I also want my life to honor and please God today. The new believers in the second chapter of Acts did not waste any time adjusting their lives to God's purposes. They are an excellent example of preparation following repentance. They wanted to be ready when Christ returned.

> **Read Acts 2:41–47. Describe the activities and attitudes of that first group of Christians, who worked together to produce godly fear in their lives.** (**Note:** *Phobos,* the Greek word for "fear," is found in verse 43. It is rendered in English as "awe" in several translations.)

Return in Complete Devotion

Initially, Malachi 4:6 may seem like an odd way to end this powerful message. But after some study, I find it appropriate. God says that Elijah's job will be to *"turn the hearts"* of the fathers and their children to each other. The Hebrew word *shuwb,* translated as "turn" in Malachi 4:6, is the exact same word translated as "return" in Malachi 3:7. See language notes below. God not only calls us to return to Him, but He also calls us to return to each other. He wants His people unified as one body, in covenant together with Him. His intention for His covenant people is that they serve and honor Him together in unity.

Malachi 4:6 then ends with a final warning. If we, as His covenant people, fail to return to a right relationship with Him, He will strike the land with a curse. (Again, check the language notes below.) In other words, if God's people do not willingly dedicate themselves and their lives to God, the day will come when God will claim their devotion. Every knee *will* bow and every tongue *will* confess.

Before we end, let's reflect once again on why our holy God deserves our fear.

Read Psalm 33:1–12. List the truths about God, as found in this passage, that should cause us to properly fear Him. (*Note: Yare'* is found in verse 8.)

I pray that this study has challenged you to commit to serving our holy God with an attitude of fear. I believe that true, godly fear is not the norm for today's Christian. You can set the example for others around you. Begin today to foster or deepen your fear of God. Remember and be completely obedient to His Word. Maintain a repentant heart, and continue to prepare your life for Christ's return. Be careful to remain totally devoted to our holy Creator, set aside for His purposes. Then your life will please and honor Him. Then you will be distinctively His— our God's treasured possession.

Then those who feared the LORD spoke with each other, and the LORD listened to what they said. In his presence, a scroll of remembrance was written to record the names of those who feared him and loved to think about him. "They will be my people," says the LORD Almighty. "On the day when I act, they will be my own special treasure. I will spare them as a father spares an obedient and dutiful child."

—Malachi 3:16–17 (NLT)

Language Notes

Malachi 4:6

English: **turn**
Hebrew: *shuwb*
Definition: to cause to return, bring back, allow to return, put back, draw back, give back, restore, relinquish, give in payment

English: **curse**
Hebrew: *cheremb*
Definition: a thing devoted, thing dedicated, ban, devotion, (appointed to) utter destruction

Notes

Week 1: God Deserves Our Fear
[1] R. C. Sproul, *The Holiness of God* (Wheaton: Tyndale House, 1985), 39–40.
[2] A. W. Tozer, *The Knowledge of the Holy* (New York: HarperSanFrancisco, 1961), 71.
[3] *Online Bible Greek and Hebrew Lexicons* (Winterbourne, ON: Online Bible, 1988–89). Applies to all language notes, unless otherwise specified. Used with permission.
[4] Willem A. VanGemeren, ed. *New International Dictionary of Old Testament Theology and Exegesis,* vol. 2 (Grand Rapids: Zondervan, 1997), 527.
[5] W. E. Vine, Merrill F. Unger, and William White Jr., *Vine's Complete Expository Dictionary of Old and New Testament Words* (Nashville: Thomas Nelson, 1996), 79.
[6] R. Laird Harris, Gleason L. Archer Jr., and Bruce K. Waltke, *Theological Wordbook of the Old Testament,* Bible Navigator Academic Edition (Chicago: Moody Press, 1980), No. 1990.
[7] Tozer, *The Knowledge of the Holy,* 15.

Week 2: God Declares His Love
[1] R. C. Sproul, *The Holiness of God* (Wheaton: Tyndale House, 1985), 109.
[2] Oswald Chambers, *My Utmost for His Highest: An Updated Edition in Today's Language,* ed. James Reimann (Grand Rapids: Discovery House Publishers, 1992), November 19.
[3] Sproul, *The Holiness of God,* 126–27.
[4] James Strong, *Strong's Greek and Hebrew Dictionary: Englishman-Strong's Concordance* (Winterbourne, ON: Online Bible, 1993), data file. No. 1586.

Week 3: God Describes a "Fearless" Life
[1] *Commentary on the Whole Bible by Matthew Henry,* ed. Leslie F. Church, New One Volume Edition (Grand Rapids: Zondervan, 1960), 1195.
[2] R. Laird Harris, Gleason L. Archer Jr., and Bruce K. Waltke, *Theological Wordbook of the Old Testament,* Bible Navigator Academic Edition (Chicago: Moody Press, 1980), No. 943.

[3]Fred H. Wight, *Manners and Customs of Bible Lands*, Bible Navigator Special Academic Edition (Austin: WORDsearch Corp., 2005), chap. 10, ebook.

[4]*The Interpreter's Bible*, vol. 6 (New York: Abingdon Press, 1956), 1125–26.

[5]Jerry Bridges, *The Joy of Fearing God* (Colorado Springs: WaterBrook Press, 1997), 99.

[6]Ibid., 98.

[7]Harris, Archer, and Waltke, *Theological Wordbook of the Old Testament*, No. 301.

[8]The Barna Group, "Morality Continues to Decay," *The Barna Update*, November 3, 2003, http://www.barna.org/FlexPage.aspx?PageCMD=Print (accessed May 12, 2005).

[9]Bridges, *The Joy of Fearing God*, 33–34.

Week 4: God's Covenant Demands Fear

[1]R. Laird Harris, Gleason L. Archer Jr., and Bruce K. Waltke, *Theological Wordbook of the Old Testament*, Bible Navigator Academic Edition (Chicago: Moody Press, 1980), No. 498.

[2]Henry Blackaby and Richard Blackaby, *Spiritual Leadership* (Nashville: Broadman and Holman, 2001), 230–31.

[3]Harris, Archer, and Waltke, *Theological Wordbook of the Old Testament*, No. 285.

[4]Association of American Publishers, Press Release dated March 6, 2006, http://www.publishers.org/press/releasecfm?PressReleaseArticleID=317.

[5]Darrell Scott and Beth Nimmo, with Steve Rabey, *Rachel's Tears* (Nashville: Thomas Nelson, 2000), 91–92.

Week 5: God Denounces Worldly Compromise

[1]*The American Heritage Dictionary of the English Language*, 4th ed. (Boston: Houghton Mifflin, 2006), http://dictionary.reference.com/browse/compromise.

[2]Ibid.

[3]Henry T. Blackaby and Melvin D. Blackaby, *Experiencing God Together* (Nashville: Broadman and Holman Publishers, 2002), 9.

[4]Ibid., 10.

[5]*Thru the Bible with J. Vernon McGee* (Nashville: Thomas Nelson, 1983), Bible Navigator software.

[6]Health Canada, "It's Your Health: Flesh-Eating Disease," http://www.hc-sc.gc.ca (accessed May 19, 2007).

[7]James Strong, *Strong's Greek and Hebrew Dictionary: Englishman-Strong's Concordance* (Winterbourne, ON: Online Bible, 1993), data file. No. 3340.

[8]Heartlight's SearchGodsWord Web site, http://www.searchgodsword.org/lex/heb/
view.cgi?number=8104.

Week 6: God Demonstrates His Justice

[1]Big Ticket Television, "Judge Judy," http://www.judgejudy.com./Episode/episode
.asp (accessed April 14, 2007).

[2]WCHS-TV8 Web site, "Judge Judy," http://www.wchstv.comsynd_prog/judy/ (accessed April 14, 2007).

[3]Michael J. Wilkins, *Matthew*, The NIV Application Commentary (Grand Rapids: Zondervan, 2004), 810.

[4]Gary M. Burge, *The Letters of John*, The NIV Application Commentary (Grand Rapids: Zondervan, 1996), 190.

[5]Ibid., 197.

[6]Ibid., 198.

[7]Thayer and Smith, "The KJV New Testament Greek Lexicon," http://www.biblestudytools
.net/Lexicons/Greek/grk.cgi?number=5401&version=kjv, No. 5401.

[8]Craig Blomberg, *1 Corinthians*, The NIV Application Commentary (Grand Rapids: Zondervan, 1994), 231.

[9]Jerry Bridges, *The Joy of Fearing God* (Colorado Springs: WaterBrook Press, 1997),
33–34.

[10]"Uses of Silver," The Silver Institute, http://www.silverinstitute.org/uses.php.

[11]Alan Robinson, *CBQ* 11 (1949): 190. Cited in Ralph L. Smith, *Word Biblical Commentary: Micah–Malachi*, vol. 32 (Waco: Word Books, 1984), 329.

[12]"Lawmaker Sued over Use of 'Jesus,'" *WorldNetDaily*, June 7, 2005, http://www.worldnetdaily.com/news/article/asp?ARTICLE_ID=44628.

[13]Josef Tson, "Suffering and Martyrdom: God's Strategy in the World,"

Suffering, Martyrdom and Rewards in Heaven (Lanham, MD: University Press of America, 1997). Printed in Ralph D. Winter and Steven C. Hawthorne, eds., *Perspectives on the World Christian Movement* (Pasadena: William Carey Library, 1981), 183.

Week 7: God Deplores "Fearless" Detours

[1]George H. Guthrie, *Hebrews,* The NIV Application Commentary (Grand Rapids: Zondervan, 1998), 445.

[2]Henry Blackaby, *Holiness: God's Plan for Fullness of Life* (Nashville: Thomas Nelson, 2003), 9.

[3]Ibid., 15.

[4]R. Laird Harris, Gleason L. Archer Jr., and Bruce K. Waltke, *Theological Wordbook of the Old Testament,* Bible Navigator Academic Edition (Chicago: Moody Press, 1980), No. 2340.

[5]Walter C. Kaiser Jr., *Malachi: God's Unchanging Love* (Grand Rapids: Baker Book House, 1984), 90.

[6]Scott J. Hafemann, *2 Corinthians,* The NIV Application Commentary (Grand Rapids: Zondervan, 2000), 369.

Week 8: God Makes Fearsome Distinction

[1]R. Laird Harris, Gleason L. Archer Jr., and Bruce K. Waltke, *Theological Wordbook of the Old Testament,* Bible Navigator Academic Edition (Chicago: Moody Press, 1980), No. 267.

[2]A. R. Williams, "King Tut Revealed," *National Geographic* 207 (2005): 16–17.

[3]R. C. Sproul, *The Holiness of God,* 2nd ed. (Wheaton: Tyndale House, 1985, 1998), 30.

[4]Matthew George Easton, *Easton's Illustrated Dictionary* (Epiphany Software, 1995).

Week 9: God Delights in Those Who Fear Him

[1]Vertical Media, "1988 Yellowstone Fires," http://yellowstoneparknet.com/history/fires.php.

[2]James Henry Breasted, *The Dawn of Conscience* (New York: Charles Scribner's Sons, 1933). Cited in *The Interpreter's Bible,* vol. 6 (New York: Abingdon Press, 1956), 1142–43.

LEADER'S GUIDE FOR GROUP STUDY

God has called you to lead your specific group at this time to fulfill His purposes. Thank you for your commitment. Your obedience will make a difference because this study encourages participants to examine their lives closely against the truth of God's Word and challenges them to make adjustments.

Your group members will need the regular encouragement and positive example you provide. May this study be an exciting time of spiritual growth for you and your group.

How to Use This Guide

In addition to discussion starters, key review questions, and summarization statements for you to use with your group, this guide provides some further application questions to help participants apply what they've learned.

In the weekly reviews, the type styles indicate how to use the material:

- *Italicized type (plain or **bold**) generally indicates instructions to the leader.*
- Plain roman type is used for material the leader may **voice to the group**: discussion starters, questions, review, and group instructions.

Week 1: God Deserves Our Fear

Review: God deserves a certain response from us because of who He is. Godly fear is a positive concept in the Scriptures. In fact, godly fear is the attitude God desires and expects.

Initiate discussion: Imagine you were invited to the White House to meet the President. Describe what you would do to prepare, how you would behave while you were there, and why.

Day 1: Fear of God Portrayed in the Scriptures

Have the group turn to table 1; then initiate discussion:
- Which of the Scriptures on table 1 had an impact on you?
- Based on this table, describe a person who fears God and one who does not.

Day 2: Deserving of Fear Because He Is Holy

Initiate discussion:
- Did you take the virtual journey?
- Did God give you a fresh awareness of His holiness and new insight this week?

Read (or ask a volunteer to read) Deuteronomy 4:10, and ask this question: According to this passage, why did God expose the people to the manifestation of His holiness at Mount Sinai (Horeb)?

Read (or ask a volunteer to read) Deuteronomy 6:1–2, and ask these questions:
- What would the presence of godly fear in the people produce in their lives?
- How would this fear take practical expression?
- Is there personal application to make here?
- After contemplating God's holiness, did you gain a new appreciation for the intercessory role of Christ? Explain.

Day 3: Fear Defined

Review language notes: Look at the original Hebrew word for *fear* and the definitions for the English words that are used to get at the meaning of the Hebrew.

Ask these questions:
- How did godly fear express itself in the lives of the Hebrew midwives?
- What do you believe it means to fear God?
- Did God use this day's lesson to reveal to you something about yourself and your attitude toward Him?

Day 4: God's Holy Nature

Initiate discussion: The Bible describes God's unique nature as holy. What does it mean that God is holy?

Review these key points:
- *Discuss the meaning of the original Hebrew word that is translated as "holy."*
- *Discuss the idea that* holy *is a general term used to describe God's nature and does not signify one single attribute.*

Ask these questions:
- Do you agree or disagree with this last idea?
- What descriptions of God's nature did you find in Isaiah 40? What did you include in your character sketch of God?

Read Jeremiah 5:20–25, and ask these questions:
- According to this passage, what is the proper response to God?
- What reasons does this passage give to support an attitude of godly fear?

Day 5: God Alone

Read Acts 17:24–28, and provide a discussion starter: Pass around a small statue, dollar bill, coin, or other item that might be symbolic of an idol, such as those worshipped in Athens during the Apostle Paul's ministry.

Describe the God that Paul introduced to the Athenians, and ask these questions:
- Have you ever or do you now worship a lesser god than the Lord God?
- Have you been guilty of limiting God? In what way?
- Have you ever had spiritual nearsightedness because you have viewed God from your own personal perspective?

Week 2: God Declares His Love

Initiate discussion: Put on the board a time line of dates from this week's study, days 1 and 2, but leave off the corresponding events. Include the years of 930, 722, 605, 586, 538, 536, 530, 520, 515, 458, 445, and 434 B.C. Challenge the class to come up with the corresponding events without looking at the study book or the Bible.

Explain importance of studying biblical history: A good grasp of biblical history will give us a better understanding of the entire Bible. This particular section of Israel's history provides the framework for the Book of

Malachi. Based on what you studied this week, where would the Book of Malachi fall on this time line? (*Ask a volunteer to mark the time line in the appropriate time slot.*)

Day 1: God's Love Revealed in History

Ask these questions, providing lead-in statements as needed:
- Did reviewing Israel's history provide you with any new insight? If so, what?
- How is God's love for Israel revealed in this history?
- God used a pagan king to fulfill His purposes for Israel. Would you share with our group an example of when God has worked His purposes out for your life in unexpected ways?
- Throughout Israel's history, we see God's full, unified nature expressed. For example, His justice with His love. Would you share an example of when you witnessed this kind of unified expression of God's nature in your own life?

Day 2: God's Love Revealed by Malachi

Ask these questions:
- Did it help to read all of the Book of Malachi in one sitting?
- What aspects of God's nature does Malachi reveal?
- What specific revelations of God's love can be seen?
- What grievances did God have with the people?
- What similar situations do we find among Christians and in the church today?

Day 3: Divine Love

Ask these questions:
- What is your response to the people regarding their doubt of God's love?
- Have you ever questioned God's love for you?
- What stood out to you about God's love as you filled in table 3?

Summarize: We can trust in God's unfailing love because it does not depend on us—it is dependent only on God's nature!

Day 4: Holy Love

Read quote from R. C. Sproul on page 35, and ask these questions:
- How does God work from the entirety of His nature and not one aspect at a time?

- How does God reveal His entire nature in the act of our salvation?

Day 5: Chosen in Love

Review: Day 5 deals with the difficult subject of God's choosing or election. It is a hotly debated topic that is not cut-and-dried. Malachi 1:2–3 tells us that God loved Jacob and hated Esau. God chose Jacob and his descendants over Esau and his descendants.

Ask these questions, reviewing the Scripture passages as needed:
- What does Romans 9:10–18 say about God's right to choose?
- What does 1 Timothy 2:3–6 reveal about the scope of God's salvation?
- What did you learn about Esau and his character from Genesis 25:27–34 and Hebrews 12:14–17?

Week 3: God Describes a "Fearless" Life

Initiate discussion: Write the following names (note: names only) for your group to view, or read the names aloud.
- Jim Anderson *(Father Knows Best, 1954–62)*
- Archie Bunker *(All in the Family, 1970s)*
- Cliff Huxtable *(The Cosby Show, 1980s–90s)*
- Homer Simpson *(The Simpsons, 1989–present)*

Ask these questions:
- What do these names have in common? *(They are all television-show dads.)*
- Can you name the television shows and when they aired?
- How do these characters differ in their roles as fathers?
- What kind of changes have occurred through the years in how the media has portrayed fatherhood?
- How do media definitions of fatherhood compare with what you learned this week in the study about the role of fathers in ancient Israel?

Day 1: Son or Servant? Yes to Both

Read Malachi 1:6–14, and review: Last week we saw that the Book of Malachi begins with God's declaration of love for Israel. This week we considered God's accusations against these people. The first accusation was that the people neither honored Him as Father nor feared Him as Master.

Ask these questions:
- Did you gain any new or renewed insight about God as Father and Master after reading the background information and the language notes for the word *honor*?
- Is this idea of God as Master new for you?

Read Romans 6:16–18, 22–23, and describe Paul's slavery analogy.
Ask these questions:
- How does this apply to Christians and their relationship with God?
- How would you describe the tension that exists between God's roles of Father and Master?
- What happens if we lean too much toward seeing Him in His Father role?
- What happens if we lean too much toward viewing His role in our lives as Master?

Day 2: Fear Deficit

Review: The people were bringing defiled sacrifices to God's altar, and the priests were accepting them.

Ask these questions, reviewing Scriptures as needed:
- According to Leviticus 22:17–25, what were God's requirements for the offerings?
- Why do you think God had set such high standards for offerings?
- Why do you think the people brought defiled sacrifices?
- What do you see in Malachi 1:6, 14 that might explain their heart attitude toward God? (*Even though the people were living in disobedience, they dared to ask God to bless them. God responded that their so-called offerings were not acceptable. In fact, the condition of their offerings revealed they, God's people, did not fear Him—and yet, even the pagan nations feared Him!*)
- How would you state Deuteronomy 10:12–13 in your own words?

Day 3: Condition of the Sacrifice

Initiate discussion: How does what was happening in Malachi's time (Malachi 1:7–8) apply to our lives today?

Review: In Hebrews 10:12, it is clear that Jesus's death was the final and complete sacrifice for sins. Therefore, sin offerings are no longer needed. However, God does require an offering from us today.

Read Romans 12:1–2, and ask these questions:
- What is the sacrifice that God requires from His children today?
- What should the condition of the sacrifice be?
- How did you do with table 4 based on Colossians 3:1–17? Did you find enough information to flesh out that table?
- Did God point out some areas in your life that need work?

Day 4: The Dishonoring of God's Name

Review: God told His people that their behavior—bringing defiled sacrifices—brought His name dishonor.

Ask these questions:
- What did we learn about the original meaning of the Hebrew word translated as "name" and the importance of names?
- How does this apply to us as Christians?
- According to 1 Timothy 6:1, what effect can our behavior have on God's name?
- In what ways do Christians today take God's name in vain?
- What about you? How do you take His name in vain?

Day 5: Sacrifices God Accepts

Initiate discussion: Connie Cavanaugh, in her book, *From Faking It to Finding Grace*, uses the term "Santa-god" to describe the place we sometimes prescribe to God in our self-centered lives. Cavanaugh says we often believe our Santa-god's job is "to satisfy our needs and most of our wants, and occasionally throw in a pleasant surprise as a bonus." Are you guilty of seeing God in that role?

Ask these questions:
- Do you sometimes forget God is holy?
- Do you ever try to take advantage of your position as His child?
- Are you giving God the first and best of your time, resources, and talents, or do you sometimes give Him the leftovers?
- According to the Scriptures we read, what kind of sacrifice does God want?

Week 4: God's Covenant Demands Fear

Initiate discussion:
- Have you ever known anyone who has had a heart transplant?
- In general, why would someone need a heart transplant, and how might it change that person's life?

Read Ezekiel 36:24–28, and discuss heart change: This passage is God's description through the prophet Ezekiel of the New Covenant that was to come and has now come through Christ. Our salvation under the New Covenant is like a heart transplant. When we enter into a relationship with God through Jesus, God begins to change who we are, what we think, how we behave, our desires, and such. Our faith will come from the inside out. It is not about mustering our will to conform to religious expectations. That was the Old Covenant. This week, we compared the Old Covenant with the New Covenant, and particularly, the priests of the Old Covenant with those of the New Covenant.

Day 1: Fear Required in Levitical Covenant

Review: This week we studied Malachi 2:1–9. God was speaking directly to His priests and Levites. He reminded them of the covenant He made with the first Levites. The covenant required godly fear from the Levites. Those first Levites were faithful to the covenant, but the current generation of Levites had broken God's covenant and misled the people.

Read Malachi 2:1–9, and ask these questions:
- Why did God establish a covenant with the Levites?
- What kind of attitude did the Levites need to be faithful to the covenant (v. 5)?
- God used the phrase "[h]e walked with me" (v. 6) to describe the faithful Levites. In light of what we learned about the original language for that phrase and in light of seeing "walked with God" used in reference to Enoch and Noah, how would you summarize the meaning of the phrase walked with God?
- What do you think that activity looks like in the life of an individual?

Day 2: Lack of Fear in New Generation

Review: We compared the original faithful Levites, who feared God, with Malachi's generation of Levites, who did not honor God's name.

Ask these questions:
- • What have you discovered about the differences between the original covenant Levites and the Levites of Malachi's day (see your table 5)?
- • Why do you think the first Levites were faithful and the Levites of the new generation in Malachi's day were not? What do you think was the root of the problem?
- • How did the behavior of the Levites of Malachi's day affect the people they were supposed to lead?
- • Why does the behavior of spiritual leaders have such far-reaching consequences?

Day 3: God's New Covenant Priests

Review the opening comments for the week 4, day 3 study.

Initiate discussion: How would you respond to the comments in the opening paragraphs of the week 4, day 3 study? Why?

Ask these questions, reviewing Scriptures as needed:
- • After comparing the 1 Peter 2 passage about the priesthood of the believer with the passage in Malachi 2 about God's covenant with the Levites, have you gained any fresh insight about the position of believers as priests?
- • According to Hebrews 9:16–28, what are limitations of the Old Covenant and the superiority of the New Covenant?
- • In light of 2 Corinthians 5:18–21, what responsibilities do we have as priests of the New Covenant?
- • *Read Malachi 2:5.* This verse says God's purpose for the covenant with the Levites was to bring life and peace. Did you find evidence in the 2 Corinthians passage that shows God's purposes for His New Covenant priests are the same?
- • How can our lives demonstrate the faithfulness of the original covenant Levites?

Day 4: The New Covenant Call

Read Psalm 34:4–10, and ask these questions:
- • What promises do we find in this passage?
- • Are there any conditions?

Read Matthew 10:16–33, and ask these questions:

- What does it mean to be *"as shrewd as snakes and as innocent as doves"*?
- As believers, what should we not fear?
- What should we fear?
- What can we, as believers, expect of God when we face dangerous or difficult circumstances as we follow Him in obedience?

Day 5: A Covenant of the Heart

Read Matthew 23:23–28, and ask these questions:
- How did the typical Pharisee approach God's law?
- How were the Pharisees in Jesus's day like the Levites in Malachi's day?

Read Hebrews 8:10, and ask these questions:
- What difference should it make in the lives of believers that the New Covenant is not written on tablets of stone like the Old Covenant?
- What is the difference between practicing religion and living a faith?
- Why is this sometimes a struggle?

Week 5: God Denounces Worldly Compromise

Initiate discussion:
- What does it means to compromise?
- What are some positive and negative examples of compromise?
- What meaning does compromise take on when we use it in the context of obedience to God?

Day 1: Uncompromised Obedience Required

Read Malachi 2:10–16, and describe the situation depicted in this passage. Ask these questions:
- How does this situation defy God's commandment found in Deuteronomy 7:1–6?
- Was the situation reported in Malachi the first time Israel had disobeyed God in this way? If not, what is another example, and what were the results?
- What are some contemporary examples of how seemingly minor compromises have led or could lead Christians to fall deep into disobedience?

Day 2: Disastrous Consequences of Worldly Compromise

Reference these Scriptures, and ask associated questions:
- *Refer to Malachi 2:10–16.* What behaviors and consequences are mentioned?
- *Read James 4:1–5.* What similarities to the situation in Malachi can be identified in James 4:1–5?
- What wise guidance does this passage in James offer those who have compromised with the world?

Day 3: Areas of Compromise

Review: When we compromise with the world, we begin to look like the world. We read a passage from Ephesians that lists many attitudes and behaviors that may show up in the lives of Christians who compromise their obedience to God.

Initiate discussion:
- Give an overall picture of what a worldly person looks like. *(Participants may refer to their table 6.)*
- How does this worldly picture stand up in light of Jesus's commandments to love God and other people?

Day 4: Corporate Compromise

Review these Scriptures, and ask associated questions:
- *Read Malachi 2:10.* What does it mean to break faith with one another?
- *Review Joshua 6–7 events.* What happened after Israel's battle at Jericho?
- What does that situation in Joshua have to do with *"breaking faith with one another"* as mentioned in Malachi 2:10?

Review Ezra 9:1–7, and initiate discussion: In the Book of Ezra, we found a situation very similar to the one described in Malachi 2:11. Ezra also reported that some of God's people had married pagan women against God's command. Even though Ezra did not personally commit this sin, he, brokenhearted before God, confessed corporate sin.
- Why do you think Ezra did this?
- What are some other examples of this in the Scriptures?
- How can an individual's sin affect the life of his or her family? His or her church?

Day 5: No Compromise!

Review and ask questions: We identified four components of dealing with sin and compromise.
- What are those four components? *(Recognition, repentance, removal, and restoration.)*
- How was the situation of compromise reported in Ezra 9–10 dealt with?
- How have our four components been put into practice in this passage from Ezra?

Review Malachi 2:15–16, and ask questions: God told the people in the same situation in Malachi to *"guard"* themselves and to *"not break faith."*
- What do these two things mean?
- How can we apply them to our own lives?

Week 6: God Demonstrates His Justice

Ask for a show of hands: Raise your hand if your life is without difficulty, trial, or suffering. Come on! Surely there is someone whose life is trouble free.

Read John 16:33, and discuss: This passage is one of numerous passages that make it clear that Christians will face trials and difficult times. In fact, in our study this week, we learned how God uses such to accomplish His purposes in our lives. We considered trials and suffering in the lives of Christians in the larger context of God's justice. Justice is an aspect of God's holy character. Remember, it works together with all the other aspects, such as love and grace. This week we see that as a holy God, He administers His justice in the lives of both nonbelievers and believers, but in different ways.

Day 1: The Certainty of God's Judgment

Read Malachi 2:17, and review: It seems ironic that after God called attention to His people's sin, they then tried to shift the blame back on God for the evil around them. "Why don't you do something about all the evil around us? Guess you just don't care!" Based on passages you studied in day 1 (Malachi, Romans 2, and Matthew 25), how would you respond to them?

Refer to Matthew 25:31–46 and Romans 8:1–4, and ask these questions:
- On what basis will Jesus separate the sheep from the goats?
- What makes the difference in outcome?

Read 1 John 4:13–18, and initiate discussion: Let's touch on 1 John 4:18 because it is so often taken out of context and used as an argument against the need to fear God.
- State this passage in your own words, and explain what we are not to fear and why not.
- What impact on our lives should the certainty of God's judgment have?

Day 2: God's Purification of His Children

Read Malachi 3:1–5, and initiate discussion: Here we see God's mercy and grace working together with His justice. According to this passage, what actions of judgment would God bring?

Review: We saw God using very similar acts of justice in the lives of believers in New Testament passages; we identified three distinct acts of God's justice. Identify those activities from these Scriptures:
- *Read Revelation 3:19. (Disciplining)*
- *Read 2 Corinthians 7:1. (Refining/purifying)*
- *Read 2 Timothy 1:8–9a. (Sharing the suffering of Jesus)*

Day 3: God's Discipline of His Children

Discuss: Define *discipline*. Discuss the two levels of meaning based on the original Greek. *(These include correcting bad behavior and training or instilling right behavior.)*

Review: What evidence did we see in the Scriptures that God's discipline of His children is temporal (does not affect eternal destination)? *(Refer to our examples of David and the Corinthian believers.)*

Read Hebrews 12:7–11, and ask these questions:
- What does God's discipline prove? What is its purpose?
- How should we respond to God's discipline in our lives?
- How do you feel about God's discipline?
- Do you feel any differently now than before completing this week of study?

Day 4: God's Refining of Those Who Fear Him

Initiate discussion:
- Define *refine* or *purify*.

- How are these different from *discipline*?

Read 1 Peter 1:6–7, and ask these questions:
- What does God use to refine our faith?
- What are some of the meanings of *trials/temptations*? *(See language notes.)*
- What different forms can these trials take in our lives?
- How do you think facing temptations and enduring trials can result in a refined faith?

Read James 1:2–4, and ask these questions:
- Why does God want to refine His children?
- What does a refined faith look like?
- Do any of you have personal experience with this that you would like to share?

Day 5: Identification with Christ's Sufferings

Read 1 Peter 4:12–19, and ask these questions:
- What does it mean to *"share in Christ's sufferings"*?
- How is this different from being refined or disciplined? What makes it unique?

Review: From Acts 5, we learned that Peter and the other apostles regularly went to the Temple to worship and share Christ with their fellow Jews. They were warned not to speak in the name of Jesus, but they were undeterred. Therefore, the Jewish leaders had them flogged. What was the apostles' response to the flogging (vv. 41–42)?

Read these Scriptures, and ask the associated questions:
- *Read John 15:18–21.* Why does the world respond to our obedience with persecution?
- *Read 1 Peter 4:1–2.* What attitude should we have about persecution (sharing in Christ's sufferings)? How should we respond?
- How does God use this kind of suffering in our lives?
- How can God use this kind of suffering in our lives to affect other people?
- Do any of you know of examples of this that you can share with the group?

Week 7: God Deplores "Fearless" Detours

Initiate discussion: Who wants to tell us about a time you took one wrong turn while driving and ended up way off course?

Review: Israel couldn't seem to stay on the right path. Even after God's discipline in exile and the amazing return of the remnant, the people again took their own road. This week we saw in our study that God still loved them. He once again called them back into a right relationship with Himself.

Day 1: The Unchanging God

Refer group to table 7, and initiate discussion: What and who do we depend on, and how dependable are they?

Read these Scriptures, and ask associated questions:
* ***Read Malachi 3:6–12.*** What does this passage teach us about God?
* ***Read Psalm 89:30–34.*** What does this passage reveal about God's nature and how He responds to us?

Review and ask questions: God may never change, but the standards of our culture and society are constantly changing.
* What are some things that our society today finds morally acceptable but that fall short of God's unchanging standards?
* Do you think most Christians' standards for their relationship with God—such as submission and obedience—meet God's standards? How or how not?

Day 2: God's Call to Return

Read Malachi 3:5–7, and initiate discussion:
* In verse 7, God called Israel to repent from their sin and return to Him in obedience. What does verse 5 give as the reason for their sin? *(For further explanation, read the quotations on page 116 from Henry Blackaby's* Holiness.*)*
* What did God promise His people if they returned?

Read Proverbs 3:7, and initiate discussion: State Proverbs 3:7 in your own words.
* How does this apply to the Israelites' rebellion?
* How far away from God do you think you have to be before there is the need to return?

- Have you ever felt God calling you to return? Will one of you share an example?

Day 3: Robbers of God

Review and initiate discussion: After God called the people to return, they asked, *"How are we to return?"* I believe they were saying, "What are you talking about? We haven't gone anywhere. Tell us even one way in which we have left You." So God gave them an example.
- What did God state in Malachi 3:8 as an example of the people's need to return?
  - Who will sum up for us God's original commandments about tithing, its purpose, and how it was used?
  - In Deuteronomy 14:22–23, what did God say was the ultimate purpose for tithing?
  - How does tithing teach this?
  - Based on the Scriptures, describe the wrong attitude or way to tithe (or give) and the right way.
  - What will be the results of giving from a proper attitude?
  - How does God not only bless the giver, but also use the giver, and why? *(This is an important concept and must not be missed. God blesses us so we will use His blessings to bless others.)*

Day 4: Repentance, the First Step Toward Fear

Read Galatians 5:16–26, and initiate discussion: Rather than asking specific questions about this day of openness to God's examination, ask participants to share whatever they will.
- Would any of you like to share about what God told you?
- Are there any other comments or questions?
- Was the day 4 study a worthwhile exercise or a waste of time?

Day 5: Obedience, the Follow-up to Repentance

Review the following Scriptures, and initiate discussion: After we acknowledge the sin in our lives and turn away from it, there is still more we must do.
- *Read Matthew 28:16–20.* Break down this passage and tell exactly what Jesus demanded of His followers.
- How is it possible to fulfill Jesus's expectations?

- *Read John 14:21–24, 31.* What does our obedience or disobedience reveal?
- How does God use our obedience?
- *Read Psalm 119:57–64.* Describe the psalmist's attitude about obedience.
- Did God show you anything this week that you need to follow through with in the area of obedience?

Week 8: God Makes Fearsome Distinction

Initiate discussion:
- Have you ever made a commitment to something—in writing—before witnesses?
- Share some specific examples. *(If answers are few, offer these examples: wedding ceremony and the signing of the marriage license; closing on the purchase of a house; contracts in which one party commits to providing a service for a set fee.)*
- What is the significance of witnesses?

Review: We studied a similar situation this week in Malachi. Those who feared the Lord came together, prayed, and signed their names to a document before God, declaring that they feared Him and honored His name. This significant event was a commitment to God and each other to remain faithful. God was pleased and distinguished this group from those who did not fear Him. Our study comes to a climax this week as God compares the two groups.

Day 1: Consumer Mentality

Read Malachi 3:13–15, and ask these questions:
- What did the people expect to get from serving God?
- What is the meaning of the Hebrew word for *gain* or *profit*?
- What did you find in Exodus 18:21 about the qualifications for Moses's helpers?
- Do you see a connection between not fearing God and seeking personal gain?

Read Matthew 16:21–26, and ask these questions:
- How does this idea of desire for personal gain show up in Jesus's interaction with Peter?

- What does it mean to deny self?
- How does this compare with seeking personal gain in serving God?
- What things do people seek to gain from the world?
- In contrast, what do we gain by following Christ?

Day 2: False Appearances

Review: According to Malachi 3:14–15, in addition to saying that serving God was futile, the people accused God once again of injustice. They said the arrogant or prideful were blessed and the evildoers prospered.

Read Psalm 73, and initiate discussion: The psalmist had similar concerns, yet he arrived at a different conclusion.
- Track the psalmist's train of thought through the psalm. What was the turning point? *(See verse 17.)*
- How does Psalm 49 put this all into perspective?
- So now how would you answer the people who accused God of injustice in Malachi?

Day 3: Roadblocks to Godly Fear

Read 2 Corinthians 10:4–5, and point out the hindrance of pride: This passage tells us that pride restricts us from knowing God.

Ask these questions:
- What did you find for your definition for pride?
- How do you think pride keeps us from knowing God?

Read Philippians 3:3–6, and ask these questions:
- What reasons for pride did Paul have?
- What are some comparable reasons that often stir up pride today?

Read Romans 12:3–8, and ask these questions:
- What is the difference in pride and humility?
- What is biblical humility?
- Have you ever been guilty of false humility? *(Reminder: False humility is an attitude that refuses to acknowledge our worth in Christ and the gifts and power He gives us in order to serve Him.)*

Day 4: The Drawing of the Line

Read Malachi 3:13–18, and initiate discussion:
- Describe the differences in attitude between the "fearless" and the "fearful" in this passage.

- How does God describe the God-fearers? The fearless?
- The people written about in the Book of Malachi had a choice to make. What was it?

Refer your group to Joshua 24:14–24, and initiate discussion: Joshua had a confrontation with Israel in which he asked them to make a similar choice.

- What was the choice that Joshua set before the people?
- What did they have to do to commit to fear God?
- How could this apply to our own lives?

Day 5: God's Remembrance of Those Who Fear Him

Read Malachi 3:16–18, and ask these questions:
- What special recognition will God give to those who fear Him?
- In the passages we read from Psalms, what other promises did we find that God makes to those who fear Him? Were any of those promises particularly significant to you?
- How did it feel to write your name in the blanks in Malachi 3:17 at the end of this week's day 5 study?

Week 9: God Delights in Those Who Fear Him

Before class, recreate the "Picture of fear" table (table 10) on a whiteboard or other display option. You will use this as you cover days 3 and 4.

Initiate discussion: This Bible study has a threefold purpose:

1. To show that fearing God is a positive biblical attitude

2. To help us better understand the meaning of godly fea

3. To instill in us a desire to commit to a life of godly fear

Will some of you share if and how these goals have been accomplished in your life?

Review: Through this week 9 study, our understanding of the eternal consequences of not fearing God and the blessings of fearing Him was reinforced. Through a review of the whole study, we were able to see a composite picture of both of these attitudes. And finally, we saw God's suggestions for fostering godly fear in our lives.

Day 1: God's Judgment Fire

Read the following Scriptures, and ask associated questions:
- *Read Malachi 4:1–3.* What will happen on Judgment Day to persons who have no fear of God? What will happen to those who do fear God?
- *Read 2 Thessalonians 1:6–10.* How could you use this passage and the Malachi passage to show that hell is a real place?
- *Read 1 Corinthians 3:10–15.* What will Judgment Day be like for believers?
- Did this day 1 study change the way you think about eternity or God's judgment?

Day 2: God's Saving Light

Initiate discussion: The day of God's coming judgment is described very differently in regard to those who fear God. What metaphor does God use to describe Himself in Malachi 4:2?

Refer to table 9 in the day 2 study, and ask these questions:
- How is Christ described?
- What are the healing results?
- Do any of you want to share an experience that illustrates the healing power of the *"Sun of Righteousness"*?

Day 3: Review: Part 1

As your class shares "fearful" and "fearless" characteristics, write them in the appropriate column on the board or display area you prepared in advance.

Explain intent: As we review the study, we will build our joint Picture of fear table. At the end, we should have a good biblical view of what it means to fear God and to not fear God.

Review the following tables and Scriptures, and ask associated questions:
- *Refer to table 1 (week 1, day 1).* What characteristics in table 1 should we add to our Picture of fear table?
- *Read Deuteronomy 4:9–14.* What was the reason for this encounter between God and the nation of Israel?
- *Read Revelation 15:4.* What should cause us to fear God? What should that fear of God produce in our lives?
- *Read Deuteronomy 10:12–13.* How would you describe a life that

fears God? *(Add these characteristics to the Picture of fear table.)*

- **Refer to table 5 (week 4, day 2).** What were the differences in attitudes between the original covenant Levites and the Levites of Malachi's day? *(Add characteristics to the Picture of fear table.)*
- **Read Matthew 10:28–33.** What should we add to the table from this passage?

Review the need for seeing God's roles in balance: Would one of you volunteer to describe the balance that should exist between God's roles as our Master and as our Father?

Day 4: Review: Part 2

Initiate discussion: Week 5 was about compromise. *(Add worldly compromise and complete obedience to table.)* Identify four components for biblically dealing with compromise. *(See week 5, day 5: recognition, repentance, removal, and restoration.)*

Review these Scriptures, and ask associated questions:
- **Read Malachi 2:16.** In this passage, what did God tell the people of Malachi to do to protect themselves from compromise? What should be added to the table about compromise?
- **Read 2 Peter 3:9–14.** In reading this passage about the reality of God's justice and judgment, what did you discover that could be added to the table?
- In what three ways does God demonstrate His justice in the lives of believers? *(Disciplining, refining/purifying, and sharing in the sufferings of Christ)*
- What do these three activities accomplish? *(Discuss and add any fearful or fearless characteristics to the table.)*
- **Read 1 Timothy 6:17–19.** How can giving God our first and best help us avoid spiritual detours and teach us to fear Him?
- **Read Malachi 3:13–18.** From this passage, we learned how God distinguishes between those who fear Him and those who do not. What characteristics found in this passage shall we add to the table?

Discuss table 10:
- Can you think of anything else we should add to this table?
- Who will volunteer to pull it together and offer a definition or description of what it means to fear God? *(Let several share their definitions.)*

Day 5: The Fostering of Godly Fear

Review these Scriptures, and ask associated questions:

- *Read Malachi 4:4–6.* Based on the definition of the Hebrew word for *remember*, what does it mean to remember God's Word?
- *Read Deuteronomy 17:18–20.* According to this passage, what benefits does reading God's Word have?
- *Read Proverbs 2:1–5.* According to this passage, what kind of attention and response to God's Word is required to understand the fear of the Lord?
- *Read Psalm 130:1–4.* How can coming to God in repentance foster godly fear?
- *Read Malachi 4:6.* This verse shows that returning to God in fearful devotion has an effect on our other relationships as well. Why do you think this is true?
- *Read Psalm 33:1–12.* One of the main points of this study is that God deserves our fear because of who He is. What reasons for fearing God can you identify from this passage?

Ask for any last comments and questions.

Ask for volunteers to share how the study has affected their relationship with God.

Ask for a volunteer to close your study in prayer.

New Hope® Publishers is a division of WMU®, an international organization that challenges Christian believers to understand and be radically involved in God's mission.
For more information about WMU, go to wmu.com.
More information about New Hope books may be found at NewHopeDigital.com. New Hope books may be purchased at your local bookstore.

Use the QR reader on your
smartphone to visit us online at
NewHopeDigital.com

If you've been blessed by this book, we would like to hear your story. The publisher and author welcome your comments and suggestions at: newhopereader@wmu.org.